THE RESERVE POLICIES OF NATIONS:
A COMPARATIVE ANALYSIS

Richard Weitz

September 2007

*****

The views expressed in this report are those of the author and do not necessarily reflect the official policy or position of the Department of the Army, the Department of Defense, or the U.S. Government. This report is cleared for public release; distribution is unlimited.

*****

I would like to thank the Beyond Goldwater-Nichols (BG-N) Project at the Center for Strategic and International Studies (CSIS)—run by Clark Murdock, Michèle Flournoy, and Christine Wormuth—for initially encouraging me to study the military reserve policies of foreign countries as part of a larger CSIS study on The Future of the National Guard and Reserves in the 21st Century. (Additional information on this project is available at *www.csis.org/isp/natlguard/*.) The Hudson Institute, directed by Ken Weinstein, and Hudson's Center for Future Security Strategies, directed by S. Enders Wimbush, has provided an exceptionally favorable environment for conducting research and writing. Several scholars at Hudson offered invaluable insights on the text. The Strategic Studies Institute of the U.S. Army War College—especially Dr. Dallas Owens, former Director of Academic Engagement—provided excellent editorial guidance and other assistance in preparing the manuscript for publication. Finally, many current and former military officers and defense experts, including individuals from some of the countries under review, graciously shared their extensive knowledge on the subject.

*****

Comments pertaining to this report are invited and should be forwarded to: Director, Strategic Studies Institute, U.S. Army War College, 122 Forbes Ave, Carlisle, PA 17013-5244.

*****

All Strategic Studies Institute (SSI) publications are available on the SSI homepage for electronic dissemination. Hard copies of this report also may be ordered from our homepage. SSI's homepage address is: *www.StrategicStudiesInstitute.army.mil*.

*****

The Strategic Studies Institute publishes a monthly e-mail newsletter to update the national security community on the research of our analysts, recent and forthcoming publications, and upcoming conferences sponsored by the Institute. Each newsletter also provides a strategic commentary by one of our research analysts. If you are interested in receiving this newsletter, please subscribe on our homepage at *www. StrategicStudiesInstitute.army.mil / newsletter/*.

ISBN 1-58487-304-3

CONTENTS

FOREWORD

While the American defense community has naturally been preoccupied with the extensive transformation of the U.S. reserve components in recent years, equally critical developments in the reserve policies of the world's other major military powers have received less attention. The inevitability of continued American engagement with these countries means that their changing policies are highly relevant to the United States. American defense planners should therefore keep abreast of ongoing alterations in these countries' reserve components and, in certain cases, might wish to adjust their own forces and policies in response.

The Reserve Policies of Nations provides a comprehensive assessment of these issues as well as a wealth of data on recent developments affecting the reserve policies of many of the world's leading military powers: Australia, Britain, Canada, China, France, Germany, Israel, Japan, and Russia. By assembling this material in a single volume, Dr. Richard Weitz and the Strategic Studies Institute hope to make it easier for readers to comprehend these changes and develop insights regarding their implications.

DOUGLAS C. LOVELACE, JR.
Director
Strategic Studies Institute

SUMMARY

Throughout the world, military reserves are changing. National governments are transforming the relationships between their active and reserve components; the allocation of roles and responsibilities among reserve forces; and the way they train, equip, and employ reservists. One central precept is driving these changes: Nations no longer consider their reservists as strategic assets suitable primarily for mobilization during major wars. Whereas previously they managed reservists as supplementary forces for use mainly during national emergencies, major governments now increasingly treat reservists as complementary and integral components of their "total" military forces.

This increased reliance on reserve components presents national defense planners with many challenges. Recruiting and retaining reservists has become more difficult as many individuals have concluded they cannot meet the additional demands of reserve service. Reservists are increasingly deployed on foreign missions at a time when expectations regarding their contributions to the management of terrorist attacks, natural disasters, and other domestic emergencies are growing. Defense planners must also continue to refine the optimal distribution of skills and assets between regular and reserve forces. Finally, national governments need to find the resources to sustain the increased use of reservists without bankrupting their defense budgets or undermining essential employer support for the overall concept of part-time soldiers with full-time civilian jobs.

Governments have adopted innovative responses to the complications associated with their growing use of reservists. To ease the pressures resulting from the increased convergence of reserve and active-duty deployment schedules, defense policymakers have tried to make rotation cycles more predictable and compatible with reservist lifestyles. In addition, the major military powers have widely adopted "total force" policies that treat their active and reserve components as integrated if not totally interchangeable elements. They have done so sometimes explicitly, sometimes just in practice, but always with major implications for a wide range of defense policies. National militaries are altering the relationship between their reserve and active-duty forces as they restructure both. Government policies increasingly treat mobilized reservists and regular forces similarly—harmonizing their organizational structures, compensation packages, and rules and regulations—as they link the two components more tightly. Nevertheless, many reservists still complain about their perceived second-class status regarding training opportunities, the quantity and quality of their equipment, and their treatment by field commanders when deployed on active duty.

The convergence in the roles and missions of countries' reserve and active components invariably raises questions over the appropriate distribution of skills between the two. Since part-time soldiers normally find it difficult to match the competencies of full-time professionals, governments have had to decide where the comparative advantages of reservists lie. Although reservists continue to perform traditional defense support functions, such as rear-area security and logistics, they have recently assumed new responsibilities. These novel tasks often reflect the special skills and assets reservists can bring from their civilian lives to their military roles. In many high-technology fields, for instance, the human resource capabilities present in a country's civilian economy exceed those readily available in the defense sector. One problem with this approach, however, is that many people join the reserves to pursue an occupation different from that of their civilian jobs. For this reason, several governments have adopted a formal policy of not requiring reservists to perform the same functions when on military duty that they do during their civilian jobs, except in emergencies.

Many countries have decided to retain certain skills predominantly in their reserve components, especially those skills they find impractical to maintain in sufficient quantity in their regular forces. For example, some medical specialties are rarely needed in peacetime, but become essential in wartime for helping severely wounded soldiers. In several cases, defense planners have assigned certain skills and missions exclusively to reservists. Although this practice helps keep costs down, the result has been a de facto globalization of the Abrams Doctrine: It has become nearly impossible for a country to go to war without mobilizing at least some of its reserve components.

Reservists are often seen as providing an essential link between a country's military profession and its civilian society. According to this view, reservists help transmit values between the two communities and limit undesirable divergences between them—an important societal concern even if few people expect the military to try to seize power through coups in the nations under study. One result of this link is that national militaries have become more susceptible to broader societal trends. In most contemporary developed countries, for example, force planners must deal with declining birth rates, a growing population too old for military service, and a decreasing interest in military careers among young adults. Widespread changes in attitudes regarding women, however, have provided military recruiters with a new source of potential enlistees.

The declining size of many national reserve components, combined with an increased tendency for both regular and reserve forces to be drawn predominantly from certain—often disadvantaged—social groups, appears to have weakened the effectiveness of this military-civilian link. In response, foreign governments have restructured their reserve components to expand opportunities for military service.

Another noteworthy development in civil-military relations has been reservists' increasingly important role in ensuring their fellow citizens' safety and security during domestic emergencies. Governments are expanding the capabilities, authorities, and missions of reservists in order to improve their ability to support civilian first responders following natural disasters, major accidents, and terrorist attacks. Officials increasingly recognize that reserve components can supply unique niche capabilities in the area of homeland security. Reservists can offer emergency responders advance military capabilities and skills without requiring governments to depend on overstretched regular forces, whose use at home could present legal and other problems. In addition, they often exhibit excellent situational awareness given their close ties to the surrounding civilian communities. As in the United States, however, foreign governments are still defining the proper roles of their militaries in the area of homeland security.

Providing these new capabilities invariably raises the financial costs of the reserve components at a time when many major military powers are trying to cut their defense budgets. National military establishments are reducing the size of both their active-duty and reserve components, but the cuts in the regular forces have typically been greater because reservists are thought to be more cost-effective. As governments spend more on training, equipping, and compensating reservists, however, the cost differential between the active and the reserve components decreases. A particularly expensive development has been the extension to reservists of health, education, and other benefits traditionally only offered to regular soldiers. With the roles of reserve and regular forces increasingly indistinguishable on the battlefield, it becomes ever harder, both morally and politically, to deny reservists perquisites enjoyed by active duty soldiers. Overcoming recruitment and retention problems among reservists has also become expensive. To fill the ranks, governments have had to employ more recruiters, fund additional advertising, and provide more generous salaries and benefits.

Governments also confront the increasingly expensive burden of sustaining employers' support for their reserve employees due to the increasing demands placed upon reservists. On the one hand, the growing time commitment demanded from reservists for training and deployments has made them anxious about potential damage to their civilian careers, especially in terms of job promotion and retention. At the same time, competitive pressures have led even strongly patriotic employers to complain about the costs of supporting their frequently absent reservist employees. Most governments have responded by both strengthening (or in some cases introducing for the first time) legal employment protections for reservists and providing greater monetary compensation and other benefits to their employers.

Still another factor that complicates determining the relative cost-effectiveness of reservists is the difficulty of evaluating the tradeoff between the lower average salary of nonmobilized reservists and the various legal and practical restrictions on their use for certain operations (e.g., the typically longer time needed for their predeployment training). It is more cost-effective to keep certain infrequently needed specialist skills predominately in the reserve components, but recent experience has shown that defense planners often underestimate their active-duty requirements for these skills. Even when adequate aggregate capacity exists, miscalculations have resulted in the frequent mobilization of certain skilled reservists, creating increasing recruitment and retention problems until governments "rebalance" their allocation of skills between the reserve and active components.

Finally, calculating the costs and benefits for the civilian economy of using reservists is even more complex. When reservists perform their military duty, employers lose their immediate services and incur costs related to hiring replacement workers as well as paying for overtime and temporary coverage. Yet, some personnel expenses decline when the reservists go on leave. In addition, civilian employers often benefit from the tangible (e.g., specialized training) and intangible (e.g., leadership) skills that reservists acquire from their government-paid training. The net effect of these disparate factors varies depending on each case. Estimating their aggregate effect across the entire national economy is considerably more complex.

The overwhelming scale of the transformation in the U.S. reserve components has diverted attention from these equally sweeping adjustments taking place in the reserve policies of other major military powers. Although many of these changes resemble those affecting the U.S. armed forces, national differences persist due to countries' varying histories, constitutional principles, human resources, economic capabilities, and threat perceptions. Since the United States will continue to engage with these military powers — in cooperation, conflict, or both — the U.S. defense community needs to keep abreast of these developments and differences. In certain cases, American defense planners might wish to adjust their own forces and policies to respond to — or even preemptively influence — changes in foreign countries' reserve policies.

CHAPTER 1

INTRODUCTION –
THE RESERVE TRANSFORMATION:
THE CHANGE TO CHANGE

Throughout the world, military reserves are changing. National governments are transforming the relationships between their active and reserve components; the allocation of roles and responsibilities among reserve forces; and the way they train, equip, and employ reservists. One central precept is driving these changes: Governments no longer consider reservists as constituting primarily a strategic asset for the "big" war. Whereas previously they managed reservists as supplementary forces for use primarily during national emergencies, they now treat reservists as complementary and integral components of their "total" military forces.

National security officials have traditionally considered their reserve components as a vital mobilization base for expanding the number of troops they could field in a major conflict. For less demanding scenarios, they viewed reservists as helping keep active-duty tours within acceptable bounds and providing regular forces time for relief, recovery, and restructuring. Although national governments today still expect reservists to augment active-duty forces and perform essential rear-area support functions, almost all of them have adopted new force employment policies that presume reservists' participation in most military activities. These tasks encompass peace operations and humanitarian disaster relief missions in largely permissive foreign environments, as well

1

as more challenging counterterrorist, post-conflict stabilization, and front-line combat operations in the world's hot zones. Since the end of the Cold War, the declining prospect of a full-scale military mobilization has led defense planners to develop more refined call-up procedures. War plans now envisage mobilizing specific reserve units or even specific individuals for each mission. When reservists sign up today, they do so with the expectation of being mobilized at least once during their period of service.

The overwhelming scale of the transformation in the U.S. reserve components has diverted attention from the equally sweeping adjustments taking place in the reserve policies of other major military powers. Although many of these changes resemble those affecting the U.S. armed forces, national differences persist due to countries' different histories, constitutional principles, human resources, economic capabilities, and threat perceptions. Since the United States will continue to engage with these military powers—in cooperation, conflict, or both—the U.S. defense community needs to keep abreast of these developments and differences. In certain cases, American defense planners might wish to adjust their own forces and policies to respond to— or even preemptively influence—changes in foreign countries' reserve policies.

Chapter 2 reviews the transformed structure and roles of the U.S. reserve components. Subsequent chapters survey some of the principal developments in the reserve policies of the world's other major military powers. Reflecting the information available, they discuss changes in the size, function, and use of their national reserve components. These chapters also highlight innovations in policies designed to increase recruitment and retention, improve relations

2

with employers, and expand the range of reserve opportunities through the creation of new categories of reservists. The concluding chapter assesses the implications of these changes and offers some considerations for U.S. policymakers.

CHAPTER 2

THE UNITED STATES

Most Americans interested in military affairs have naturally focused on the revolutionary transformation occurring within the U.S. armed forces. Since the end of the Cold War, the size of both the U.S. active and reserve components have declined by approximately one-third. At the same time, American military personnel have experienced a sharp increase in their operational tempo. Reservists were seldom used during most of the Cold War, supplying on average less than one million days of duty annually before the August 1990 Iraqi invasion of Kuwait. By 2003, however, the members of the U.S. reserve components were providing 63 million days of duty per year. The average length of a reservist's tour of duty has also reached levels not seen in over half a century — exceeding 300 days on average in recent years. This surge began in the 1990s with the U.S.-led military interventions in Somalia and the former Yugoslavia,and from 1996 to 2001, members of the U.S. reserve components annually provided on average about 12.5 million days of duty per year. The recent wars in Afghanistan and Iraq have made clear the extent to which the U.S. reserve components were being employed as an operational rather than strategic force.[1]

As in other countries, the U.S. military reserve structure reflects the nation's distinct historical origins, security requirements, and constitutional principles. The U.S. Department of Defense (DoD) is unique, however, in having seven major distinct reserve components within its subordinate military departments. The Department of the Army contains two reserve components: the U.S. Army Reserve and the Army National Guard. The Department of the Air Force includes two reserve components as well: the Air Force Reserve and the Air National Guard. The Department of the Navy has three reserve components: the Navy Reserve, the Marine Corps Reserve, and the Coast Guard Reserve, which falls under Navy control in wartime. Since U.S. states and territories lack their own navies and the Marine Corps is too small to sustain a federal force structure, the U.S. Constitution authorizes only the Army and Air Force have state-based National Guard components. The relatively large number and diversity of these structures make it likely that certain foreign practices could provide insights and lessons for at least some U.S. reserve components.

The September 11, 2001 (9/11), terrorist attacks underscored the vital contribution of reservists in supporting American civil authorities and homeland defense. The authoritative 2005 *Strategy for Homeland Defense and Civil Support* called for greater "attention on better utilizing the competencies of the National Guard and Reserve Component organizations" in these missions.[2] The members of the National Guard are widely deployed throughout the United States, sometimes even working as emergency responders in their localities. For centuries, they have assisted communities stricken by natural disasters. In addition, Title 32 of the United States Code grants the National Guard unique legal privileges in operations on U.S. territory. For instance, Guard members operating in both Title 32 and state active duty status can legally undertake a much wider range of domestic law enforcement activities than regular federal forces (which are governed by Title 10).[3] Finally, while DoD officials have insisted that almost all U.S. regular forces must train and equip primarily for combat operations, National Guard leaders have evinced somewhat more interest in developing certain dual-capable units optimized for both all-hazards homeland security emergencies and overseas military missions.[4]

Since 9/11, federal and state leaders have mobilized thousands of reservists as part of Operation NOBLE EAGLE — the post-9/11 campaign to maintain air sovereignty over the United States — and other domestic counterterrorist missions. Members of the Air Force Reserve and the Air National Guard conduct approximately three-fourths of the flying missions for NOBLE EAGLE.[5] The Army National Guard (ARNG) has created new units to help operate the U.S.-based elements of the evolving ballistic missile defense architecture. The ARNG is also establishing 55 Weapons of Mass Destruction-Civil Support Teams (WMD-CSTs), at least one in each U.S. state and territory. Each WMD-CST consists of 22 highly trained specialists who, like all Guard members, can be federalized in an emergency. Although limited by their small size and lack of organic long-distance transport, these teams can help emergency responders detect threatening chemical, biological, and radiological/ nuclear (CBRN) agents and provide advice on how to respond. The ARNG is also creating a dozen CBRNE Enhanced Response Force Packages (CERFPs) within the United States.[6] These 120-member units include medical, chemical, engineering, and rescue teams trained to help manage the consequences of a range of catastrophes. The Congress has sought to enhance the effectiveness of state national guards by allowing them to establish a National Emergency Assistance Compact (EMAC). This arrangement enables state governments to receive help from National Guard units in other states on an expedited basis. The difficulties in responding to Hurricane Katrina in August 2005 led to widespread discussion about possibly expanding the military's role in domestic emergencies unrelated to acts of terrorism. Consequently, DoD has since augmented the planned role of military reservists in responding to future natural disasters.[7]

Even before Katrina, Operation ENDURING FREEDOM (OEF) in Afghanistan and neighboring regions revealed major problems with the way DoD managed its reserve components.[8] For example, some small businesses and self-employed reservists have suffered undue income loss, while mobilized reservists have encountered unequal compensation, inadequate healthcare, and other difficulties.[9] DoD systems for tracking reservists (especially members of the Individual Ready Reserve), as well as their skills and experience, have also proved inadequate to the challenge. These data management difficulties have contributed to an excessively long and unresponsive mobilization process. Operation IRAQI FREEDOM (OIF) has exposed further problems, including the inadequate training, equipping, and funding of U.S. reserve components.

The prominent reserve presence in OIF — as of November 2005, 40 percent of all U.S. forces fighting in Iraq belonged to the reserve components[10] — has ensured widespread awareness of these deficiencies. The subsequent public criticism reinforced internal pressures within DoD to change long-standing policies in its reserve components. The definitive 2006 *Quadrennial Defense Review* (QDR) *Report* acknowledges that the "strategic reserve" approach of the Cold War is largely outdated. In its assessment, "The Reserve Component must be operationalized, so that select Reservists and units are more accessible and more readily deployable than today."[11] The magnitude of the ongoing transformation of the U.S. reserve components becomes evident when one considers that they represent almost half of all American military personnel.

Each of the military branches has launched various initiatives to optimize the contributions of their reserve components to the new security challenges of the 21st century. For example, the Army Reserve has identified "Six Imperatives" to guide its transformation efforts: reengineering the mobilization process, transforming command and control, restructuring units, improving human resources, building a rotational-based force, and improving individual support to combatant commanders.[12] Under its recently implemented Federal Reserve Restructuring Initiative (FRRI), the Army Reserve has begun reducing its nondeploying force structure by cutting headquarters staffs and consolidating training and command structures.[13] Through the 2005 Base Realignment and Closure (BRAC) process, the Army Reserve is eliminating or realigning a higher percentage of facilities than any other component. All its 125 new Armed Forces Reserve centers will be shared with a reserve component from at least one other military service. To reduce the length of required pre-deployment training and elevate the collective preparedness of its members, the Army Reserve has adopted a new Army Reserve Training Strategy of "train-alert-deploy" in place of the Cold War-era model of "alert-train-deploy."[14]

All these measures aim to buttress the new Army Force Generation (ARFORGEN) model. The concept employs a force rotational model that assumes sustained Army Reserve deployments will remain a feature of U.S. military operations for the indefinite future. It seeks to generate, train, and equip Army Reserve "force packages" capable of deploying to a theater of operations for up to 1 year during any 5 year period. The corresponding cycle for the Army National Guard envisages one deployment window every 6 years. According to former Army Chief of Staff General Peter Schoomaker, the aim of these complementary rotation systems is to generate 18-20 Brigade Combat Teams (BCT) "indefinitely."[15] When not mobilized for missions, regular and reserve Army units cycle through various phases of refitting, retraining, and reequipping. Army Reserve force planners anticipate that the predictability of the ARFORGEN will make its deployment obligation more acceptable to reservists, their families, and their employers.[16]

The Army is also adopting a new modular structure for both its active and reserve components. By more effectively mixing and matching active and reserve units, the reorganization would create a rotational pool of some 70 BCTs and 200 Support Brigades. At present, Army planners intend to field 117 modular brigades in the Regular Army, 106 in the Army National Guard, and 58 in the Army Reserve.[17] The Army Reserves have established an "Individual Augmentee Program" to supplement this new system of rapidly deployable modularized units. An associated Worldwide Individual Augmentation System will make it easier for the combatant commands to access Individual Augmentees with needed skills.

The Navy and Air Force, which began to experience force structure stress during the U.S.-led military interventions of the 1990s, adopted new deployment systems based on rotating "force packages" even before the Army. Among other objectives, these systems attempt to make active and reserve deployments more predictable, especially for enduring "steady-state" operations. Even in the absence of another major war or other national emergency, all three Services expect to rely on their reserve components to help meet at least some of their routine operational requirements.

Besides these separate Service initiatives, DoD has sought to make its reservists more effective by enhancing their capacity to operate jointly with members of the other military branches. The intent is to extend the level of "jointness" now achieved among regular forces to the reserve components. In recent years, increasing numbers of reservists have served on joint staffs and in joint billets.[18] The National Guard Bureau (NGB), a federal body that administers U.S. Government programs involving the state Army and Air National Guard forces, has led many of these efforts. Although still focused on the needs of the Army and Air Force, the NGB has established direct ties with the Joint Staff and combatant commanders to address their reserve requirements. In addition, the NGB has collaborated with other DoD bodies to develop joint doctrine, education, training, and exercises for issues related to homeland security. Its newly established Joint Continental United States Communications Support Enterprise (JCCSE) links many of these commands to state, local, and federal government homeland security stakeholders. In addition, the NGB has consolidated the three previous guard headquarters in each U.S. state, territory, and the District of Columbia into a single joint force headquarters for each location. An important function of these streamlined bodies is to help provide reservists with more opportunities to enroll in joint professional military education courses — either residential or through Internet-based distance learning — as well as to acquire joint duty experience.[19]

DoD has sought to make reserve assets more rapidly available for operations by shortening the time required for their mobilization. At the same time, then Secretary of Defense Donald Rumsfeld in 2003 directed the Department to end the active component's dependence on reserve mobilizations during the initial phase of any rapid military operation. To this end, the Department has begun reducing the disproportionate concentration of certain skill sets in the Reserve Components. In the U.S. Army, for instance, at the end of January 2004 when the "rebalancing" process had just begun, approximately 60 percent of the combat structure, 54 percent of the combat support structure, and 69 percent of the combat service support structure resided in the Army Reserve and Army National Guard. In some areas, the disparities were even starker. At that time, some 97 percent of the Army's civil affairs units, 72 percent of psychological operations units, 72 percent of the hospitals, and 70 percent of medical units belonged to the Army Reserve alone.[20]

As of March 2006, the Army Reserve was still providing 96 percent of the Army's civil affairs units and two of the Army's three Psychological Operations groups—as well as 30 percent of the Army's total combat support and 45 percent of its combat service support capabilities.[21] The Army Reserve and Army National Guard also retain primary responsibility for support functions relating to homeland security, information technology, logistics and transportation, military police, and protection against CBRN agents.[22] Since many of these occupations draw on specialized civilian skills that would be expensive to duplicate widely in the regular forces, it might prove prohibitively expensive to rely solely on regular forces and reserve volunteers during even the first weeks of major military operations.

These disparities reflect the historical legacy of the so-called "Abrams Doctrine." General Creighton Abrams, Chief of Staff of the U.S. Army from 1972-74, allegedly placed certain essential military assets in the Army Reserve and Army National Guard in order to make it difficult for the United States to fight another Vietnam-scale military operation without mobilizing the reserves. His intent was supposedly to discourage U.S. presidents from launching major wars that would lack widespread popular support. Due to their different histories, smaller sizes relative to their corresponding regular components, and recent rebalancing efforts, the reserve components of the Air Force, Navy, Marine Corps, and Coast Guard contain a more balanced mix of capabilities that complement the assets resident in their respective active-duty components. Nevertheless, the Air Force depends on volunteers from its reserve components to supply certain flight crews and maintenance personnel required to keep two of its Aerospace Expeditionary Forces (AEFs) readily available for routine 90-180 day deployments. The Air Force Reserves also provide about half of the Air Force's aggregate strategic airlift capacity.[23] The Navy similarly relies on its reservists to provide most of its military intelligence, fleet support airlift, and coastal warfare capabilities.[24]

Through rebalancing the mix of tasks and capabilities between the active and reserve components, DoD has sought to ensure that the regular forces possess sufficient organic assets to initiate any operation without large-scale mobilization of the reserve components (which would also have the undesirable consequence of alerting potential adversaries of the impending military action).[25] In particular, the military services have sought to augment certain high-demand/low-density (HD/LD) combat support and combat service support assets hitherto found largely in their reserve components. This process has involved both creating more regular units with these capabilities and transferring military personnel from lesser-used military specialties to these overstretched fields. According to official data, the military branches have rebalanced approximately 70,000 positions within or between the various active and reserve components. The services intend to rebalance more than 50,000 additional military personnel by 2010.[26] The 2006 Air Force and Navy Posture statements review their rebalancing achievements as well as their recent efforts to increase integration between their Services' active and reserve components (e.g., the creation of a USAF Total Force Integration Directorate).[27] The Army Posture statement similarly highlights its "rebalancing" of capabilities between Army Regulars and Army Reservists.[28] Even after these changes, however, the U.S. military will continue to rely on the reserve components for most large-scale operations, especially during the post-conflict reconstruction phase. Any occupation force will need personnel with skills widely available in the civilian world such as civil affairs, psychological operations, military police, civil engineering, and medical and dental care.

DoD policymakers have also proposed changes in legislation to improve the Department's access to its reserve components, especially for potential homeland security missions. The Bush administration has requested that Congress amend Title 10 USC 12304 (the Presidential Reserve Call Up Authority), which enables the activation of reserves without a declaration of a national emergency to supplement the available volunteers in the event of a natural disaster.

The administration desires to extend the maximum length of active duty service under this authority from 270 to 365 days. It also desires greater legal flexibility to access the consequence management capabilities resident in the reserve components to support U.S. civil authorities during a domestic emergency (defined as a "serious natural or manmade disaster, accident or catastrophe").[29]

CHAPTER 3

THE UNITED KINGDOM

Like their American counterparts, British defense officials now recognize that the United Kingdom Reserve Forces (RF) will participate in most military operations rather than solely as a last resort to counter direct threats to British territory. A July 2004 Ministry of Defence (MOD) report states, "Our Reserve Forces have evolved from a large but little used force to one that is ready and capable of providing an integrated component of Defence, structured to support more frequent expeditionary operations either as individual reinforcements in key specialist areas, or as formed sub-units."[30] Starting with the interventions in Kosovo and Bosnia, the RF have participated in most British combat and peace support operations during the past decade. Current MOD force employment policy, which reflects a new "culture of mobilization," anticipates that RF members will be called up for active duty at least once during their service commitment. Britain also adheres to a "total force" concept that holds that reservists should be treated indistinguishably from active-duty troops when they work together on operations.

The British reserves consist of two main components: the Regular Reserve and the Voluntary Reserve Forces (VRF). Regular Reservists are former members of the Regular Forces who are still liable for compulsory mobilization. For example, discharged Regular Army personnel are required to join the Army Regular Reserve, subject to diminishing obligations with age. Regular Reservists primarily constitute a standby rather than a ready reserve. The British government no longer expects to mobilize them except in times of national emergency (though the MOD did recall 420 Regular Reservists for service in Iraq in 2003). The main Regular Reserve components are the Army Reserve; the Royal Air Force Reserve (RAFR); and the Royal Fleet Reserve (RFR), which consists of former Royal Navy and Royal Marine regulars. Each Regular Reserve component also has a small contingent (typically ex-regulars) who volunteer to extend their reserve liabilities.[31]

The training and mobilization obligations of Regular Reservists depend on such factors as their age, sex, and length of regular service. They fall into one of four main categories. First, members of the Officer Reserve have a compulsory training obligation of 4-6 years after leaving regular or reserve service. Second, Regular Reservists are subject to compulsory training for as many as 6 years after their discharge. Third, members of the Long-term Reserve have completed their Regular Reserve obligation, have no additional training obligation, and serve until they reach 45 years of age. Finally, military pensioners are former active-duty personnel who have completed "pensionable service." They have a legal liability for recall up to the age of 60 without a training obligation. For financial and other reasons, some former active-duty members also join the VRF after leaving regular service, giving them a dual reserve status.[32]

The government now relies primarily on the VRF for most deployments. VRF members commit to at least 27 days of training each year, though some specialist units, whose civilian and military skills often overlap, have a minimum commitment of only 19 days. Their training commitment typically entails 1 night per week, 1 weekend per month, and 2 weeks of continuous duty each year. This "annual camp" occurs either at a military training establishment, as an attachment to a regular unit, as part of a formal military exercise, or a combination of these elements. Since the 2-week training often provides the only opportunity for the entire reserve unit to train together, reservists are expected to take leave from their regular job to participate. The MOD offers extra volunteer training opportunities to reservists who wish to acquire special skills. The Ministry also periodically uses reservists' training time to deliver actual military support (e.g., manning operational centers, unloading ships, or evacuating medical casualties from overseas) for overstretched regular forces. Although this practice provides reservists with more realistic training, it can deprive them of opportunities to exercise other basic skills.

Approximately 40,000 members currently serve in the VRF. Some 85 percent of them consist of people who have joined the Territorial Army (TA) directly from the civilian community. Along with members of the Army Reserve, TA volunteers comprise the main part of the Army Ready Reserve. The remaining part-time voluntary reservists belong to the Royal Naval Reserve, Royal Marines Reserve, and the Reserve Air Force. Some VRF members have previously served on active duty, though this is not required. Certain members of the Regular Reserve join the VRF to keep their military skills sharp through its requirement for periodic training. The duration of reservists' period of mobilization varies but typically ranges from 3-12 months, which includes time for pre-deployment training, post-deployment leave, and reintegration into civilian society.

The size of the British reserve components has declined in recent years, along with a corresponding decrease in the number of active-duty personnel. According to annual editions of *The Military Balance*, compiled by The International Institute for Strategic Studies, the number of British reservists fell from 340,100 in 1990, to 302,850 in 2000, to some 272,500 in 2005. In comparison, the size of the active-duty forces declined from 306,000 troops in 1990, to 212,450 troops in 2000, to almost 206,000 troops in 2005. As of early 2007, Britain had 191,030 regular forces and 199,280 reservists. Of the reservists, 134,180 were in the Army (1,030 on active duty); 22,200 in the Royal Navy (720 on active duty); and 42,900 in the Royal Air Force (360 on active duty). The TA's authorized strength amounts to 42,000 personnel, including a University Officer Training Corps (UOTC) of 3,500, but recruiting and retention problems have left it with a force of only 37,360. At present, there are also 2,100 reservists serving in Northern Ireland.[33] Although the UOTC provides many TA officers, its 19 university-based units cannot be mobilized except during a national emergency. The Royal Navy sponsors 14 University Royal Navy Units at or near university campuses. These units allow undergraduates to gain insight into Navy careers without any service obligation. The 15 University Air Squadrons offer undergraduates an opportunity to fly training aircraft for some 20-30 hours a year.

The Territorial Army has changed substantially during the past century. When the United Kingdom created the TA in 1907, the term "territorial" signified that its members — who had previously been organized into separate elements such as the Volunteers, Militia, and Yeomanry — were not required to serve outside British territory. With the end of conscription in 1960, however, the relationship between the TA and the Regular Army changed dramatically. Whereas in

World War I, World War II, and the Korean War the TA consisted of complete combat divisions, in 1967 the MOD introduced a "One Army" concept that integrated the TA units directly into the Regular Army.[34] The new policy required the TA, when mobilized, to provide "round out" units of up to battalion size to support the active-duty Army. (The U.S. Army National Guard adopted a similar policy after the Vietnam War.) The One Army concept also established for the first time a single chain of command for Regular and TA personnel.[35]

In March 2006, Armed Forces Minister Adam Ingram announced plans to enhance the TA's contribution to future military operations by aligning its structure and roles more closely with those of the regular Army. These changes will occur as part of a broader Future Army Structure (FAS) initiative, which aims to create new medium-sized fighting units. Within the FAS framework, TA members will enjoy greater opportunities to train with their Regular counterparts, making it easier to integrate reservists when mobilized. Under the new "pairing" concept, each TA unit will have affiliations with two Regular units: a primary affiliation with the unit that it would join in operations, and a secondary affiliation with a unit with which it will conduct routine training. (The current "regimental" system combines one regular battalion and one TA battalion into a British Infantry regiment.) In addition, the TA will continue transforming its large combat units into either combat service support units or into individual or small-size reinforcement components for integration directly into regular units engaged in military operations short of large-scale warfare. Specifically, the new TA units will include more engineers, armored, intelligence, and other support forces, and fewer infantry, signalers, logisticians, and volunteer medical troops. The remaining TA infantry will be reorganized into 14 TA infantry battalions that will constitute an integral part of the Future Infantry Structure. Additional full-time staff will become responsible for acquiring, training, and keeping new recruits. These changes are intended to be budget neutral. They also are scheduled to take place over a number of years to allow TA members time to transfer to new skills or units.[36]

The Royal Naval Reserve (RNR) and the Royal Marines Reserve (RMR) represent the Royal Navy's reserve components.[37] Entrants into these groups must be between the ages of 16 and 40 and either British or Commonwealth citizens, or Irish Republic nationals. They must meet the same entry standards as those joining regular Royal Navy components. The RNR no longer controls its own ships or has its own operational units. Its members typically provide additional trained personnel to the Royal Navy in times of heightened operational commitments. They train in support fields such as logistics, medicine, and communications. About a quarter of RNR members have previously served in the Royal Navy. Opportunities exist for RNR personnel to serve with the Royal Navy for periods of up to several years while retaining their reserve status. Provided a mobilization order is not in force, RNR members may resign with 1 month's notice. In peacetime, RNR members normally undertake a minimum of 12 days of Operational Role Training (ORT) annually, complemented by a number of evening drills and some weekend drills. Most new entrants attend evening drills once a week at their nearest RNR Unit. Specialized short-term (2 weeks or less) training courses for RNR members are provided by the relevant Royal Navy training schools.

The Royal Marines Reserve (RMR), consisting of almost 1,000 trained personnel, is a formal component of the Royal Navy. Approximately 10 percent of RMR members serve at any one time as long-term volunteers in regular Royal Marines units deployed in conflict zones such as Afghanistan or Iraq. Other RMR members augment the Regular Marines Corps on a short-term basis. Since RMR personnel are expected to integrate readily with their regular counterparts, they must pass the same challenging Commando Course, which normally requires 8-to-10 months of training. Volunteers may be civilians with no previous military experience, transfers from the TA, or former active-duty Royal Marines. Like new TA members, RMR entrants typically undergo specialist training at the Reserves Training and Mobilisation Centre opened at Chilwell in 1999.

The Reserve Air Forces numbers slightly over 40,000 personnel. Most serve in the Royal Air Force Reserve, providing either full or part-time service to fulfill their obligations as former members of the Regular Royal Air Force (RAF). The Royal Auxiliary Air Force (RAuxAF) is another fully functioning element of the RAF. The RAuxAF is staffed by approximately 1,500 part-time, volunteer military personnel who normally hold full-time civilian jobs. The 20 RAuxAF units, most of which are co-located at operational RAF stations, provide many essential specialist and support functions. These contributions encompass intelligence, air traffic control, linguistics, medical services, and other noncombat functions. The MOD called up RAuxAF units during both the 1990-91 Persian Gulf War and the current global war on terrorism.

In order to make the reserve components more flexible and allow individuals greater opportunities to define their level of commitment, the Reserve Forces Act of 1996 established several other categories of reservists. These components differ both in terms of their functions and in the levels of commitment required by reservists. The MOD envisages taking further steps to develop a flexible continuum of service, including expanding opportunities to move among the various reserve and active duty components. In its December 2003 defense white paper, the government affirmed: "Our strategic intent is for Reserves to be a part-time but professional force, underpinned by a strong volunteer ethos. . . . We aim to achieve this by encouraging the widest possible participation through offering as much flexibility in the types of Reserve as possible, while meeting Defence needs."[38]

The MOD provides certain reservists the opportunity to volunteer for Full-Time Reserve Service (FTRS) for a predetermined period in a specific billet with the active-duty forces. Individuals volunteering for FTRS typically fill established regular positions during manning shortfalls. FTRS Reservists are fully deployable, both overseas and in the United Kingdom. FTRS has three sub-categories, which vary by commitment. Those on Full Commitment serve world-wide in the same manner as their regular counterparts. As an example, the Royal Navy allows its reservists to serve with active-duty units on full-time contracts for time periods ranging from three months to three years.[39] Those on a Limited Commitment are available for deployment for up to 35 days annually, though they are restricted to 21 days in any one period. Those on Home Commitment cannot be deployed or detached without their consent, except for essential training. The MOD encourages employers to grant sabbatical leave for reservists on FTRS.

Additional Duties Commitment (ADC) Reserves are reserve personnel who serve part-time, often on various job-sharing arrangements, for a specified time period in a particular post. The minimum commitment for an ADC Reservist is at least 1 day a week of continuous service for at least 13 weeks. Such reservists can work in either regular or reserve units. Most individuals with ADC status work at various military headquarters.

The category of Sponsored Reserves represents a British innovation designed to deal with the increased importance of private sector support workers in sustaining military operations. Sponsored Reserves are civilian contractors who have agreed to join the reserves to facilitate their integration into the British armed forces. In peacetime, they perform support services, from providing transportation to maintaining increasingly complex weapons systems, through their civilian employers. During conflicts and crises, Sponsored Reservists are liable for mobilization and deployment in support of ongoing military operations. The MOD now conditions the awarding of several large contracts on the condition that a certain percentage of a contractor's workforce joins the reserves. Each contract specifies the length and frequency of their call-up commitments, as well as their conditions of service (e.g., some continue to receive higher civilian rates of pay). The Sponsored Reserves concept aims both to save money (where civilian contractors replace more expensive military personnel) and increase deployability (by requiring civilians to accept reserve status). In Iraq, some 1,500 Sponsored Reservists served in uniform. They have supported the RAF's Mobile Meteorological Unit, the Navy's Ro-Ro Strategic Sealift Vessels, and the RAF Royal Squadron of transport planes and helicopters.[40] Unfortunately, the MOD has applied this concept in an incomplete and piecemeal manner.[41]

The High Readiness Reserves category consists of people who have specific skills that the military expects to need urgently in a crisis, but rarely otherwise. They agree that the MOD can mobilize them with less than 1 week's notice and retain them on active duty status for a maximum of 9 months. If they work more than 2 days a week in regular civilian jobs, their employers must sign an annual agreement consenting to their participation in the High Readiness Reserves.

In accordance with its Defence Planning Assumptions, the British government assigns three primary military roles to the reserve components.[42] First, they augment active-duty forces during long-term operations such as the peacekeeping and humanitarian missions in Bosnia, Kosovo, and Sierra Leone. When combined with the demands of operations in Northern Ireland, Afghanistan, and especially Iraq (where over 40,000 British troops were deployed at one time), these enduring commitments have made it necessary for many regular British soldiers to serve on back-to-back operations with only 9 months between deployments.[43] By providing an additional source of manpower, reservists allow regular personnel time to recuperate. The MOD tries to rely on voluntary mobilization for such long-term operations, but can compel RF activation if necessary. Through their participation in Joint Civil-Military Co-operation Groups and other mechanisms, British reservists in the Balkans and Iraq have assisted with physical reconstruction, reviving commerce, and promoting good relations among local parties.

Second, the Reserve Forces provide the MOD with additional capability for large-scale military operations. In these cases, the RF supply both individual reinforcements (often through "back-filling") and entire formed units. Their main function is to augment the force pool available for British commanders as well as to provide a foundation for regenerating an even larger military such as the force Britain established during both world wars. In any major conflict, moreover, the reservists would provide essential specialist capabilities. The 1998 Strategic Defence Review, while mandating that regular forces maintain sufficient capacity to undertake early-entry operations independently, assigned reserve and contractor personnel a greater role in providing combat support and combat service support units for large short-notice missions. For example, the restructuring enhanced the TA's role in such areas as artillery, air defense, and medical services while decreasing its contingent of infantry and engineers.[44] Since 2003, over 12,000 reservists have deployed on Operation TELIC, the British component of the coalition military mission in Iraq and its surrounding areas. This mobilization required the largest compulsory call out of Britain's RF since the 1956 Suez Crisis. Overall, reservists have contributed 11-12 percent of the total British military contingent in Iraq.[45]

Finally, even in smaller operations, the MOD relies on the Reserve Forces' specialized capabilities that the Regular Forces find impractical to maintain in sufficient quantity to meet all possible contingencies. Some specialist skills and training—such as those of civilian professionals with expertise in foreign languages, information technologies, or other fields—are available primarily or exclusively in the reserve components. For instance, the Territorial Army has units consisting only of specialists in such areas as computers, medicine, and engineering. In Operation TELIC, the TA provided approximately half of the deployed medical personnel for Britain's field hospitals.[46] They have also proved useful in managing major civilian infrastructure projects in environments too dangerous for civilian contractors. The MOD is developing an improved database of reservists' civilian skills to utilize them better in future contingencies — though with recognition that many reservists, especially outside the medical profession, join the military in part as a change from their civilian jobs.

British reservists also assumed a more prominent role in maintaining security within the British homeland. The MOD expects VRF personnel, who are based at hundreds of locations across the United Kingdom, to provide important military support during domestic emergencies. These contingencies include major terrorist attacks, natural disasters such as major flooding, or disease outbreaks such as the 2001 Foot and Mouth epidemic among British livestock.[47] In particular, the government can now mobilize the 14 regional Civil Contingency Reaction Forces (CCRFs), which became fully operational at the end of 2003. These units consist of approximately 500 Volunteer Reservists drawn from all military services. Their function is to provide, on request, Military Aid to the Civil Authorities (MACA) after a large-scale terrorist attack, catastrophic accident, major natural disaster, or similar nonindustrial emergency (i.e., the authorities cannot use the reserves to break strikes) within the United Kingdom.

In any major incident, Regular Forces are expected to lead the response because of their generally greater capabilities and readiness. The CCRFs, however, could offer rapid if temporary general support in such areas as reconnaissance, access control, food, and shelter. They could also quickly make available their command, control, and communications assets to local responders. CCRF members have begun training alongside their local emergency responders, who would provide the main medical, fire, and other more specialized assistance. The MOD's assumption is that, in certain cases, unarmed CCRF members could usefully supplement both the regular forces and first responders by drawing on their local knowledge and contacts gained from living and working in the affected region. To enhance reservists' ability to respond to domestic emergencies, the MOD now requires all VRF members to undertake additional training in MACA-related tasks. For example, contingency planning exercises help familiarize reservists with emergency management procedures, organization, and services. CCRF volunteers undertake 5 days of supplementary training and all other VRF members undergo 2 additional days of MACA-related training.[48] Since the prospects of any particular CCRF unit being mobilized at any one time are low, and they are not expected to remain on duty beyond the immediate emergency, CCRF volunteers retain their normal reservist roles and responsibilities.[49]

In all these functions, British policy treats the reserve components as an essential—and perhaps increasingly important—link between the military and civilian society. Whereas recent budget cuts have led to the closure of many regular military bases, reservists remain stationed at approximately 400 bases throughout the country. In particular, TA units are much more widely dispersed than Regular Army forces, making them the most visible face of the British armed forces in many places. Their long-standing ties with local communities also facilitate the recruitment of new members to both the Reserve and Regular Forces.[50] For example, the TA directly supplies a large percentage of recruits for the Regular Army.[51] Like the members of other reserve components, TA members are employed in a wide variety of civilian sectors and often hold leadership roles in local communities.

The Reserve Forces Act of 1996 makes all reservists subject to compulsory mobilization both in national emergencies and in support of military operations outside the United Kingdom, including humanitarian missions and post-conflict stabilization operations. The MOD has a formal policy of "intelligent selection" under which it generally first solicits volunteers for any reserve operation before requiring compulsory mobilization. Since the VRF has many members who have served in active-duty status, the MOD plans on mobilizing them first in time of war or emergency. The Ministry intends to mobilize the Regular Reservists only when the relevant VRF resources have been exhausted or when the required capability does not exist within the VRF. When mobilization becomes necessary, the Defence Secretary issues a Call-out Order that specifies which reserve components are mobilized and for what purpose.[52] Before the 1996 Act, the government had to mobilize the entire VRF component. The problems the MOD experienced with this requirement in the early 1990s convinced the British government to adopt new legislation that permits individual call-ups.

In accordance with the transformation of Britain's reserve components into an operational reserve, the United Kingdom has devoted considerable attention to improving their training. For example, the MOD recently established a Tri-Service Reserve and Mobilisation Training Centre in Nottinghamshire dedicated to preparing mobilized reservists for operations.

All reservists receive some pre-deployment training at this center or at facilities run by the individual military services. The TA has 13 specialist units whose members have skills of particular use to the military, such as the Royal Logistics Corps and the Royal Electrical and Mechanical Engineers. These units recruit throughout the country, but train centrally and with less frequency than most TA units. Nonspecialized units have traditionally recruited and trained locally. In early 2004, however, it became evident that some local recruiters had allowed new entrants to join the TA even when they had failed to meet its medical or physical fitness standards. Consequently, the MOD has begun to exercise greater central supervision.[53]

The MOD tries to arrange for reservists to spend at least some time training with those regular units they would join on deployments, but such integration has not always proved possible. In addition, surveys show that reservists still complain that their training needs receive lower priority than those of their regular counterparts. Specifically, they cite less flexible training schedules, training classes that are cancelled at the last minute or that address a narrower range of skills than those offered regular forces, fewer opportunities to train with the latest military equipment, and field commanders' frequent lack of knowledge of the particular training and skills reservists bring to an operation. The MOD has taken steps to overcome these problems. For example, it has lengthened the average mobilization period from 9 to 11 months for reservists deployed in Iraq to provide opportunities for additional training.[54]

The MOD relies on various measures to sustain employer support for their employees' increasingly burdensome reserve commitments. All new reservists are expected to inform their employers of their enlistment.[55] The MOD regularly solicits employer opinions on reserve-related issues through research, direct contact, and the National Employer Advisory Board, which provides independent advice to the MOD on issues regarding reserve employment. The SaBRE (Supporting Britain's Reservists and Employers), a MOD-initiated program launched in October 2002, seeks to strengthen employers' support for the reserve components, especially the VRF. Through disseminating information and promoting a consultative dialogue among employers, reservists, and government bodies, SaBRE highlights the transferable technical and managerial skills reservists acquire through military service that could benefit civilian employers. The program also offers examples of best-practice policies and solicits the views of employers and reservists regarding employment issues. SaBRE staff cannot intervene directly to resolve employer-reservist problems, but they can provide guidance regarding both parties' precise legal obligations and details about where to obtain legal, financial, and other assistance.[56] The MOD also recently established a network of regional Employer Support Executives that, along with the Reserve Forces and Cadets Associations (formerly the Territorial and Auxiliary Volunteer Reserve Associations), work directly with civilian employers on reserve issues.[57]

The Reserve Forces Act limits the time for which any reservist may be mobilized. The law generally allows for a maximum cumulative total of 12 months in any 3-year period. In practice, the MOD seeks to restrict reserve mobilizations to a maximum of 12 months every 5 years since feedback from reservists and their employers indicate that a one-in-five year deployment schedule is more acceptable.[58] On the other hand, surveys indicate that reservists complain if they lack opportunities to participate in actual military operations when suitable opportunities arise. For this reason, the MOD tries to keep them "simmering" by mobilizing at least a proportion of the reserves whenever possible.[59]

To make reservists' commitments even more tolerable to their families and employers, the MOD aims to mobilize only those reservists who volunteer for a deployment. In addition, during the week after a reservist receives a call-up notice, moreover, the MOD allows an employer to request that the planned mobilization of an employee be delayed or cancelled if the reservist's absence would inflict "serious harm" on the business or organization. Employers can also receive financial assistance to offset any costs incurred as a result of a call-up. These could include the costs of advertising for a replacement, overtime pay, or the need to hire temporary employees. In recent years, the MOD has increased these benefits and streamlined the application procedure required to access them.

Although the Reserve Forces Act does not specify an obligatory notice period, the MOD intends whenever possible to give 28 days formal advanced warning of mobilizations. This length corresponds to the 4-week notice employees generally give their employers when leaving a job. The MOD also seeks to provide additional informal early warning of possible deployment when possible, though this increases the risk of reservists, their families, and their employers preparing for mobilizations that do not occur. The recently instituted Employer Notification procedure requires new VRF members to grant the MOD permission to contact their employer directly, ensuring their awareness of their employees' possible mobilization.[60] Previously, reservists had to report their civilian employment to the MOD but were not obliged to inform employers of their military status.

Furthermore, employers are not required to pay a mobilized reservist his or her salary. The MOD pays VRF members an annual bounty, a tax-free bonus for fulfilling their training commitment, and a salary for each hour of training plus any related expenses. When they are called up for active duty service, they receive the same salary as Regular soldiers according to their rank. In April 2005, the MOD adopted a new remuneration package specifically targeted at deployed reservists. If a mobilized reservist earns more in his or her civilian job than in the reserves, the MOD will make up the shortfall within very generous limits. If this salary supplement proves insufficient and the reservist can demonstrate hardship, he or she can apply for additional compensation. The Safeguard of Employment Act of 1985 obligates employers to rehire former employees who have been mobilized, provided the employee returns to work within 6 months of his or her demobilization. The Act requires the employer to reinstate returning reservists on the same terms (but not necessarily in the same position) as they would have enjoyed if they had not been mobilized. British law also prohibits employers from dismissing an employee solely or mainly because of that individual's reserve status.

The increasingly generous benefits provided to British reservists have left the MOD uncertain regarding the actual costs of its reserve components. A complicating factor is that many defense expenditures apply to the British armed forces as a whole and cannot easily be disaggregated into expenses for particular regular and reserve components. Even more difficult to assess are the relative marginal costs of using a regular soldier or a reservist for any particular task.

Since 2003, the war in Iraq has had the same negative effects on Britain's reserve components as it has on those of the United States. Although many reservists express satisfaction with their opportunity to serve their country by participating in actual deployments, all Britain's VRF components are below their authorized strength and suffer from higher turnover than desired. Despite a costly advertising campaign and extra compensation for reservists called up to active duty, the Territorial Army in particular has suffered major recruitment, retention, and readiness problems. In 2005, the TA had only 35,000 soldiers—its smallest size since its creation in 1907 and well below its authorized size of 42,000. According to press accounts, in practice only 24,000 of these troops have been fully trained, of which at most 12,000 are available for deployment to Afghanistan, Iraq, and the Balkans. Since the beginning of the Iraq war in March 2003, the rate of exodus from the TA has more than quadrupled, to some 6,000 for the 1-year period ending in September 2005. A vicious circle has set in, with the TA's shrinking size reinforcing warnings about "overstretch," further weakening the appeal of reserve duty.[61] These concerns about overstretch appear warranted. Although the MOD intends for the TA to provide only 10 percent of the personnel deployed on overseas missions, in 2004 reservists comprised almost a quarter of the British military contingent in Iraq.[62] Altogether, about a third of current TA personnel have already served tours in the Middle East or Afghanistan.[63] According to the provisions of the 1996 Reserve Forces Act, the MOD cannot legally require them to serve again for another 3 years. Given that the Iraq war resulted in the first compulsory call-up of reservists from all three services since the Korean War, officials fear that other reserve components besides the TA could suffer similar mobilization problems.

The MOD is still evaluating how best to structure and use Britain's reserve components to manage contemporary security challenges. It has launched a major study of possible further reconfigurations in the TA—"Future Army Structure: Territorial Army," scheduled for completion in 2012—as part of a larger assessment about how to optimize the British military for 21st-century security requirements. A major challenge consists in strengthening the integration of reserve and regular personnel while still providing opportunities for those who want to limit their military commitments. Demographic problems common to many countries (e.g., a smaller number of young people fit for military service) also worry defense planners. Although the Ministry of Defence would like to restrict the use of most reservists to only large-scale operations, Britain's extensive overseas security commitments and personnel shortages in key skills could require the continued use of many reservists for smaller-scale operations. MOD officials hope that their recent changes in reserve structures and policies will help resolve this problem. In the end, however, the next British government, like many of its 20th-century predecessors, might consider more radical solutions to re-balance the country's ambitious foreign policy objectives with its limited military capabilities.

CHAPTER 4

FRANCE

The end of the Cold War and the increased prominence of new international security threats have resulted in a major restructuring of the French armed forces. The disappearance of the Warsaw Pact eliminated France's need for a large standing army consisting primarily of short-term conscripts. The growing importance of peace-and-stability operations and antiterrorism missions has increased the requirement for more professional soldiers available to serve on long overseas deployments. In response to these changed conditions, the French government has substantially reduced the size of its active-duty forces. More importantly, in 1996 President Jacques Chirac decided to end conscription, a long-standing bulwark of French defense policy dating back to the French Revolution. In October 1997, the French legislature adopted a Law on National Service Reform (No. 97-1019) that suspended conscription for the indefinite future. The last French Army conscript ended active duty in November 2001.[64]

The formation of France's new all-volunteer professional armed forces has required an equally far-reaching transformation of the country's military reserve system. At the height of the Cold War in 1984, France's military reserve pool exceeded four million men. In case of a war with the Warsaw Pact, French planners expected to call up half a million reservists.[65] After mobilization, reservists would have comprised almost half of the Army and over one-third of the Air Force.[66]

In October 1999, the French government adopted law No. 99-894, the fundamental purpose of which was to transform the French reserve components from a *"réserve de masse"* (mass mobilization reserve) to a *"réserve d'emploi"* (deployment reserve). As part of this effort to convert the reserves from a large manpower pool to a smaller but better integrated operational component of the French military, the legislation created two separate reserve components: *la réserve opérationnelle* (the Operational Reserve) and *la réserve citoyenne* (the Citizens' Reserve).[67] Reservists in both components must be French citizens, physically fit, have no criminal record, and be at least 17 years old. (A 2006 law lowered the age limit from 18 years.) All reserve positions are open to women. The maximum age of entry into the reserves for individuals lacking military experience is 30 years. Former regular soldiers can enter later, with the maximum age varying according to their past rank. Reservists normally end their term of service when they reach the age of 40 years (for enlisted personnel) or 50 years (for officers and noncommissioned officers).[68]

The *réserve opérationnelle* is designed primarily to provide trained reinforcements for the active-duty forces. Its members consist of both former active-duty military personnel and volunteers. Upon discharge from active service, all French military personnel are required to serve an additional 5 years in the *réserve opérationnelle*. Volunteers can serve from 1 to 5 years, depending on the terms of their *contrat d'engagement à servir dans la réserve* (ESR). This renewable contract also specifies the voluntary reservist's military field and specialization. Periodic reserve training typically amounts to 20-30 days per year, up to 120 in case of overseas operations. Units in the *réserve opérationnelle* can be used both in France and abroad, in war or peacetime. Units of the *réserve opérationnelle* are expected to "bring a quick response to operational needs. One third of the reservists will be ready for use within 4-15 days.[69] During a crisis, their duties include providing general reinforcement, aiding the population, and maintaining continuity of essential public services. In times of "extreme emergency," the government can also use reservists for internal and border security, including protecting public facilities.

With the creation of the *réserve opérationnelle*, the French government is moving toward the same "total force" concept embraced by the United States and many other Western powers. In the past, reservists formed a separate branch of the French military.[70] Today, members of the *réserve opérationnelle* join a specific military branch (Army, Navy, *gendarmerie*) as indicated in their ESR contract. They are also able to serve in the same missions as regular military personnel, though typically for a shorter time period. They can participate either as individual members of an active-duty unit or — less commonly, especially on overseas missions — as a collective military unit consisting only of operational reservists. While on active duty, reservists enjoy the same status and financial compensation as regular personnel of comparable rank and grade. French defense officials anticipate that better integration of the *réserve opérationnelle* into the active-duty military will improve its readiness, interoperability, and usability.[71]

Law No. 99-894 describes the main purposes of the *réserve citoyenne* as maintaining a link between the French nation and its armed forces as well as providing "*l'ésprit de défense*" ("the spirit of defense") to the French people.[72] In effect, this new reserve component represents an effort to sustain the sense of national solidarity that many believe existed during the era of compulsory military service. The *réserve citoyenne* includes three groups. The first category comprises former military personnel who did not receive a summons to join the *réserve opérationnelle*. The second group consists of former members of the *réserve opérationnelle* who have finished their service obligation but wish to remain a formal part of the French armed forces. Civilian volunteers constitute the third element of the *réserve citoyenne*.

The different reserve categories share many duties, including assisting with recruiting, facilitating communications between the public and the armed forces, reinforcing emergency response mechanisms, and organizing ceremonies designed to mark important military events. Originally, Law No. 99-894 allowed the armed forces to integrate members of the *réserve citoyenne* into the *réserve opérationnelle* in times of war or crisis. In April 2006, however, a modification to the legislation restricted the use of the *réserve citoyenne* to "nonmilitary tasks" only.[73] At present, the military neither assigns these reservists to a specific post nor provides them with formal military training, military uniforms, or regular stipends. The government still hopes, however, that the *réserve citoyenne* will provide a pool of potential volunteers for entry (or in some cases re-entry) into the *réserve opérationnelle*. French law makes such transfers fairly routine. In their activities, the members of the *réserve citoyenne* fulfill some of the representational and public education functions performed by the U.S. National Guard, while lacking its combat and combat support responsibilities.

A 2002 report issued by the National Assembly, the lower house of the French legislature, found that almost all reservists had previously served in the active-duty military.[74] These findings evoked concern since, with the suspension of national service, the number of former conscripts would decline over time. As a result of this study, the French government took steps to increase the number of voluntary enlisted members, including allocating more funds for their recruitment. At the end of 2004, France had 43,614 volunteers in the *réserve opérationnelle*, only a slight shortfall from the desired target of 44,270.[75] Current force goals envisage reaching 94,000 volunteers by 2012: 29,000 for the army, 7,700 for the navy, 8,250 for the air force, 40,000 for the *gendarmerie*, 8,600 for the medical corps, and 500 for the energy corps.[76] By 2015, French officials hope to have 100,000 reservists, with half of them in the *gendarmerie*.[77] Although the French government had initially sought to create an all-volunteer military reserve force, the April 2006 legislation acknowledged the value of retaining former active-duty personnel in the *réserve opérationnelle* because of their superior training and availability.[78]

That approximately 50 percent of all French reservists will serve in the *gendarmerie* testifies to its increased importance in defending the French homeland. In 2000, the *gendarmerie* accounted for only 27 percent of the Reserve.[79] Although this paramilitary force falls under the authority of the Ministry of the Interior in peacetime, it works closely with the Army command, enjoys high interoperability with Army units, and is funded through the defense budget as "an integral part of the armed forces." In wartime, the *gendarmerie* reports to the armed forces command, doubles in size, and fulfills priority homeland defense and security missions.[80] The *gendarmerie* has sufficient armored vehicles, helicopters, and crew-serviced weapons to respond to large-scale terrorist incidents or to reinforce regular military forces in an emergency. It has two main components as well as several specialized units. One particularly important specialized unit is the *groupement de securité et d'intervention de la gendarmerie nationale*, which has unique capabilities for countering WMD terrorism involving chemical, biological, and nuclear/radiological agents.

The *gendarmerie* has two main components, the *gendarmerie départementale* and the *gendarmerie mobile*. The *gendarmerie départementale* provides the main police force outside major metropolitan areas, where the *police nationale* has primary jurisdiction. In the remaining 95 percent of French territory, the *gendarmerie départementale* helps regulate traffic, investigate crimes, track down suspects, and maintain aviation and port security. In frontier regions, the *gendarmerie départementale* also assists with border control and the enforcement of French immigration laws.

The other component, the *gendarmerie mobile*, has the lead role in combating terrorism within France. It gathers intelligence about possible terrorist attacks, promotes public safety, and protects the country's critical civilian infrastructure (including airports, dams, the Paris Metro, foreign embassies, national monuments, and both France's civilian nuclear plants and its nuclear weapons).[81] The reserves in the *gendarmerie* have less legal authority than their regular counterparts. For example, they can use their weapons only in "cases of legitimate defense."[82] Despite this restriction, *gendarmerie mobile* reserves played a major security role during the 2003 G-8 summit at Évian. (The Army reserves also participate actively in homeland security endeavors — providing security at special events and helping manage natural disasters such as storms, floods, and forest fires.[83])

The *gendarmerie* is involved in all overseas deployments by virtue of its traditional military police duties. Its specialized units also assist with peace operations, intelligence gathering, and other foreign missions. Article 8 of Law No. 99-894 also permits the use of members of the *réserve opérationnelle* on *operations extérieures* ("external operations," or OPEX) outside French territory. From the point of view of the United States and France's other potential military allies, this policy change represents a major improvement. The French law banning the use of conscripts in foreign combat zones considerably limited France's ability to contribute to the 1990-91 DESERT STORM campaign. In the past, France has had to rely on the French Foreign Legion and other units consisting solely of full-time soldiers for operations outside French territory. Although French conscripts did participate in the 1954-62 war in Algeria, their use provoked widespread controversy despite Algeria's formal legal status as a part of France.[84] The difficulty associated with using conscripts on foreign operations contributed to the decision to end conscription and to transform the military into an entirely professional force capable of responding to international contingencies as well as direct threats to French territory.[85]

Most French reservists who deploy overseas possess special skills (e.g., linguists, jurists, and engineers). Article 9 of law No. 99-894 allows for such specialists to enter the reserves without prior military training. They often work in civil affairs (*actions civilo-militaires*), a particularly important function in the post-conflict stability operations that increasingly preoccupy Western militaries.[86] Although French military planners seek to take advantage of the skills reservists gain through their civilian employment, they recognize that many reservists join the armed forces to do something different from their regular jobs. To encourage more volunteers, French authorities do not require reservists to use their civilian skills in their military assignments.

In practice, however, the participation of French reservists in foreign operations has remained limited. In 2002, only some 350 reservists were engaged in overseas military missions.[87] In 2003, OPEX constituted merely 3.94 percent of all reserve activities. The corresponding figure for 2004 was 3.92 percent.[88] French legislation indicates that the main function of reservists is to enhance security within France and substitute for active-duty units deployed abroad. For example, the 2003-08 military program law states that the reserves "will have to fulfill missions at home, as a complement or substitute for operational personnel occupied elsewhere, and thus constitute a pool at the disposal of the government according to arrangements defined in an inter-ministerial framework, for the support of civilian/military operations as well as protection and security operations at home."[89]

In 2004, approximately 1,000 French Army Reservists served on such *opérations intérieures* ("internal operations," or OPINT).[90] These included both homeland defense missions under Plan Vigipirate and responses to forest fires and other natural disasters under Plan Hephaistos. The Vigipirate civil defense plan is a unique French creation. Under its provisions, which have remained in force since the start of Operation DESERT STORM in January 1991, the police, *gendarmerie*, and other branches of the French armed forces conduct joint domestic operations to ensure the protection of the country's critical infrastructure. These security forces increase their patrols, reinforce border crossings, and enhance their protection of the country's schools, public buildings, and other sites vulnerable to terrorist attacks.[91]

In the past, restrictions on the allowable duration of reserve mobilizations have also discouraged their overseas use. Until recently, the maximum amount of time that a reservist could serve on active duty was only 120 days. Reservists also had to obtain employer approval 2 months in advance of deployment. As a result, the Ministry of Defense found it difficult to dispatch reservists overseas for sufficiently long periods to make their deployment worthwhile. To allow for greater use of reserve forces in foreign engagements, the French legislature in April 2006 amended law No. 99-894 to extend the permissible mobilization period to 210 days in case of war or emergency. It also reduced the required time for advanced notice in such circumstances to 1 month.

While the French military has met its goal for recruiting reserve officers, its recruitment of reserve enlisted personnel has lagged, probably due to the priority given to manning the new all-volunteer active-duty force. To achieve the 2008 objective of 68,000 reservists under ESR, a 6,000 per year increase of the enlisting will be necessary. Thus far, the 2008 target objective has been fulfilled at 73 percent and 47 percent for officers and non-commissioned officers, but only at 23 percent for ordinary non-officers, even if the number of rank and file reserve recruits has increased 44 percent since 2002.[92] Before 2003, officers made up 60 percent of the reserves, noncomissioned officers (NCOs) about 30 percent, and enlisted members only 10 percent. The government would like to have 25 percent officers, 30 percent NCOs, and 45 percent enlisted men by 2008.[93] In order to facilitate the recruitment of enlisted personnel into the reserves, the French government has increased the signing bonus for volunteer recruits. Any reserve recruit that registers to become an enlisted soldier between 2003 and 2008 will receive a 1,000 euro bonus.[94] This measure and related initiatives helped increase the number of enlisted soldiers in the French reserves by 24.73 percent in 2004.[95]

To increase the overall number of reservists, especially volunteers, the French government has revised other recruiting techniques. For example, French authorities began requiring all French youth— males since 1998; females since 2000—to participate in a *journée d'appel de préparations à la défense* (JAPD, a "day of introduction to military service"). The JAPD obligates all French citizens between the ages of 16 and 18 to spend a day at a nearby public facility (often a military base) at the government's expense. Upon arrival, they learn from regular and reserve soldiers about the French defense establishment, including opportunities to serve in the military. Only those who complete the program receive a *certificat individuel de participation*, which is required to register for the national examinations administered by public entities (e.g., to enter a public institution of higher education or to obtain a government job). Participation in JAPD is also required for entry into the reserves or other components of the French armed forces. Another measure intended to increase awareness of the reserves was the institution (in Article 55 of Law No. 99-894) of a *journée nationale du réserviste*. On this day, the national government sponsors nationwide ceremonies paying tribute to France's reservists and highlighting their contributions to French security and society.[96] Other reserve recruiting efforts include targeted information campaigns at universities, academic gatherings, and professional meetings (e.g., among medical specialists).[97]

France is having the same difficulty as other countries in securing employer support for the increased use of reservists. Employers complain about absent workers and lower profits, arguing that France's reserve policy weakens national firms against foreign competitors. Although law No. 99-894 permits reservists to serve for up to 30 days annually, it only requires their employers to grant them 5 days of military-related leave per year. Reservists need their employers' specific approval, negotiated at least 1 month before their service begins, to miss any additional work days. Reservists typically must devote many weekends and holidays to fulfill their reserve commitments.

Growing employer discontent led the government to create a *Conseil Supérieur de la Réserve Militaire* (CSRM) in October 2000 to provide a forum for elite discussion concerning the reserve components. Its 62 members include members of parliament, armed forces personnel, major employers, and representatives of various reserve associations. The CSRM is charged with promoting reform of the reserve components and helping maintain good relations among civilian employers, the armed services, and the government. The CSRM is also responsible for sustaining the "*ésprit de défense*" in France. To this end, the CSRM produces an annual report analyzing how the implementation of different laws affects the reserve components. Recent CSRM projects have included creating a database of competencies within the reserves and establishing conventions that give reservists more benefits than guaranteed by law (such as more compensation and shorter employer notification requirements).[98] Survey data show that employers generally appreciate that reservists bring valuable skills acquired on duty to their workplace. On balance, they believe that reservists have a positive effect on their business.[99] In an effort to increase this support, the government in December 2005 passed a law providing a tax credit to employers of up to 200 euros per reservist, or 30,000 euros in total, to help compensate for the financial costs of employing reservists.[100] Thanks to the creation of the CSRM and these other initiatives, French authorities have made some progress in achieving improved relations among employers, reservists, and the state.[101]

CHAPTER 5

GERMANY

Unlike most other North Atlantic Treaty Organization (NATO) countries, Germany stubbornly adheres to a policy of military conscription. At present, the Compulsory Military Service Act subjects all male German citizens to conscription into the German armed forces (the *Bundeswehr*) when they reach the age of 18. The typical duration of conscription is 9 months, but conscripts can subsequently volunteer for several additional (typically, 2-13) months of service. As a result, the *Bundeswehr* contains both career forces (mostly officers, NCOs, and specialists) and *Zeitsoldaten* (soldiers who serve for limited periods before returning to civilian life). *Zeitsoldaten* encompass soldiers performing their basic military service as required by law, those who have voluntarily extended their initial tour, and members of the *Bundeswehr's* reserve components.

Many German military and civilian leaders believe that conscription fulfills an essential function in keeping the armed forces firmly connected to the general population and, since 1990, in helping to integrate former East German citizens. In this regard, they stress that one of the roles of the reserves is to represent the military to society. For example, the German Ministry of Defense's most authoritative publication on the country's reserve components states: "Reservists are mediators between the *Bundeswehr* and the civilian sector of society. They contribute to sustaining motivation for military service and help people to see security issues in a wider context."[102] Partly because of Germany's complex history, the country's leaders repeatedly emphasize the importance of the country's reserve components as "citizens in uniform."

Opponents of conscription see compulsory military service as an unnecessary infringement on civil liberties now that the Cold War has ended. In addition, the large number of draft exemptions generates complaints that the arbitrary burden of military service falls disproprotionately on certain strata of German society, violating the constitutional principle of *Wehrgerechtigkeit* (justice in military service). Critics also cite pragmatic considerations against compulsory military service. In particular, they maintain that conscription wastes defense resources in training and equipping large numbers of short-term soldiers that are unlikely to be used in a conflict—and will perform poorly if they are forced to do so.[103]

A major factor sustaining conscription is that its elimination would deprive the public sector of the extraordinarily large number of individuals who perform low-paid community services as an alternative to military service (the *Zivildienst*). Each year over 100,000 Germans, approximately half the total number of draftees, choose to work for 10 months in retirement homes, community service organizations, and international development projects. The ease with which potential conscripts can declare themselves conscientious objectors has effectively transformed Germany's system of universal conscription into one of universal public service, at least for young men. A further factor sustaining conscription is the fear that ending it could hurt military recruiting—already threatened by declining birth rates. The *Bundeswehr* regularly recruits about one-half of its career personnel from its conscripts. Finally, some Germans, concerned about the increased participation of German military units in foreign operations, have offered a version of the Abrams doctrine. Since the *Bundeswehr* consists largely of conscripts rather than professional soldiers, they expect that politicians will avoid using it excessively or without democratic consent.

The German government considers anyone who has ever served in the military, either through universal service or by volunteering, as a reservist. In peacetime, former servicemen are liable for military service as reservists after a 12-month waiting period (*Schutzfrist*) following their discharge from active duty. They remain subject to call up until they reach the age of 60 years for officers, 45 for NCOs, and 32 for regular soldiers (60 years in the case of emergency). Regular soldiers who have to leave active duty because they have reached the maximum retirement age can be recalled until the age of 65. The time requirements for female personnel are shorter.

At present, Germany has 245,702 active-duty troops: 160,794 in the Army, 24,328 in the Navy, and 60,580 in the Air Force. The reserve components consist of 144,548 soldiers, 3,304 sailors, and 13,960 Air Force personnel — for a total of 161,812 reservists.[104] The German government conducted an extensive defense policy review in 2003. The resulting *Defense Policy Guidelines* stressed the need to restructure the *Bundeswehr* into a more agile force focused on multilateral conflict prevention and crisis management operations rather than on defending against a conventional attack.[105] The most recent German government plans, adopted in January 2004, envisage a *Bundeswehr* with approximately 252,500 active-duty troops by 2010.[106] This force will consist of 35,000 front-line troops, suitable for high-intensity operations; 70,000 "stabilization" soldiers intended for humanitarian and post-conflict reconstruction missions; and 147,500 support troops, 39,000 of whom will undergo civilian vocational training at any one time. The *Bundeswehr* planned for 2010 will also contain some 55,000 conscripts, as well as approximately 80,000 reservists, integrated with the active-duty troops.[107] There will also be 2,500 reserve duty training slots.[108]

The government can call up most reservists for 15 days of training per year. Reservists with special military-relevant skills tend to be called up most frequently, while reservists with unneeded skills may never be recalled to active duty. The limited time available for reserve training requires most reservists to acquire their skills elsewhere—either during their terms of active service or from their civilian employment. The system emphasizes individual training and command post exercises, especially for reserve officers and NCOs. Officers are normally liable for periodic training call-ups for a 10-year period, NCOs for 7 years, and all other enlisted personnel for 4 years. People with valuable skills not widely available in the military may be subject to periodic call-ups for longer periods. The German defense budget includes specific reserve training slots to pay for these call-ups. Each slot equates to 365 duty days. For example, the 1993 budget authorized 4,000 reserve training slots. This allocation paid for an average of 4,000 reservists on active duty at any one time that year, or over 100,000 individual call-ups. At the height of the Cold War in the early 1980s, the budget authorized 35,000 slots.[109] In Fiscal Year 2004, the German government allotted 2,200 reserve training slots, which funded 805,200 individual training days (including reservists participating in missions abroad).[110] The number of training days required of reservists in peacetime depends on their career category. Reserve officers typically have the highest requirement, whereas enlisted personnel have the lowest. Although the *Bundeswehr* affirms its right to mobilize any reservist in an emergency, it seeks to use only volunteers for most operations.[111]

German military doctrine assigns several important roles to the country's reservists. First, they allow the *Bundeswehr* to reconstitute a large force if Germany were again threatened by a conventional attack. For example, reservists would provide the bulk of the officers and soldiers for the army's large number of "semi and nonactive units." These formations, maintained at low readiness in peacetime, have as their primary mission both national and collective defense (e.g., of Germany's NATO allies).

Second, the German government expects that some reservists will volunteer to help manage the consequences of domestic and international emergencies, including natural disasters.[112] In this regard, the German government has recently expanded the responsibilities of its reserve components in meeting terrorist and other homeland security threats to Germany's population and critical infrastructure. According to current doctrine, "Although this is first and foremost a task to be filled by internal-security forces, the armed forces will be available to act, within the scope of the law in force, whenever they alone possess the capabilities needed or when the protection of the citizens and of critical infrastructure can only be provided by the *Bundeswehr*."[113]

Finally, reservists can both backfill for active-duty forces deployed in foreign missions and participate directly in foreign operations if necessary. During the past decade, German military forces have been involved in several foreign operations. In July 1994, the Federal Constitutional Court ruled that the German Armed Forces could participate in multinational military operations within a United Nations (UN) framework. The *Bundeswehr* subsequently sent substantial armed contingents to the Balkans. In August 2003, Germany assumed command of the International Security Assistance Force (ISAF) in Afghanistan. In the summer of 2006, 780 German soldiers participated in the 2,000-man European Union Force (EUFOR) for the Democratic Republic of Congo, which reinforced the 17,000-strong UN peacekeeping force supervising the country's national elections. This deployment marked the first time German peacekeepers have taken part in a UN operation in Africa.

Besides participating in peacekeeping operations, Germany's membership in NATO might require using military force to defend another alliance member—a scenario that arose in 1990 and 2003 with the possibility of an Iraqi attack on Turkey as well as after the 9/11 terrorist attacks, when NATO invoked its Article 5 commitment to defend the United States. Germany's international commitments might require sending reservists abroad to augment active-duty forces. The Ministry of Defense recognizes that reservists can bring linguistic skills, overseas experience, and other valuable qualifications to foreign operations.

Germany has three categories of reservists.[114] The Reinforcement Reserve (*Verstärkungsreserve*) consists primarily of volunteers for general assignments. The Manpower Reserve (*Personalreserve*), which encompasses most specialists, consists entirely of volunteers who fill specific short-term vacancies and other temporary assignments. The General Reserve (*Allgemeine Reserve*) includes all "nonassigned reservists" who are subject to mobilization in a national emergency. They provide a general manpower pool, with no predesignated mobilization positions. Some reserve personnel are also defined as "deployment reservists." In return for extra compensation during peacetime, they maintain a high readiness level by performing special exercises and at least 72 days of military service within a 3-year period. These measures aim to enable them rapidly to reinforce active-duty forces, including for homeland defense and foreign missions.

Reservists are placed in a category as soon as they have completed their active-duty service. They are assigned according to the same standards used for active forces. Their civilian qualifications and experience are also considered. In principle, Germany uses the same criteria to select and train its regular and reserve components. These troops train together whenever possible to facilitate their integration. Reservists with homeland security tasks coordinate their training and exercises with German civilian agencies having similar responsibilities. The military uses reservists to supplement and assist the regular forces on whatever scale is needed—from employing single reservists to integrating whole reserve units. At present, the *Bundeswehr* does not plan to mobilize complete reserve units except on rare occasions.[115]

Currently, the *Bundeswehr* is attempting to make the recruitment, mobilization, and use of reservists easier and more effective. The *Bundeswehr Reservist Concept* observes, "A modern personnel management tailored to the individual will have an immediate effect on the reservists' willingness to perform military service prompted especially by long-term planning, taking personnel and professional matters into consideration, a modern training programme, attractive career opportunities and timely publication of information."[116] The German military works closely with the private sector to gain access to reservists with useful civilian skills and qualifications. German planners recognize that reservists can provide advanced skills and specializations more widely available in the civilian economy than in the armed services.

The Ministry of Defense also sponsors many events and initiatives to integrate the reservists into the regular armed forces. The Ministry's *Dezernat Reservistenarbeit* (Department of Reservist Work) assists active-duty soldiers who volunteer to continue as reservists after their term of service ends. The department formally functions as a mediator between the *Bundeswehr* and society. It manages a discussion forum among *Zeitsoldaten* and offers academic courses on subjects considered useful to the military or German society. The semi-official *Bundeswehr* Reservist Association serves as an umbrella organization for all interested active and former reservists. Funded by the federal government, the Association has offices staffed by full-time employees throughout Germany. It encourages voluntary reservist work outside the *Bundeswehr*, thereby promoting integration of reservists into civilian society.[117] Participation in Association activities provides reservists with additional opportunities to serve beyond the limited number of active duty billets available to reservists.[118]

In compensation for their service, reservists are paid for the time they spend in training and receive free meals, accommodations, equipment, medical treatment, and other benefits. In accordance with the Conscripts and Dependence Maintenance Act, reservists employed in the private sector receive compensation for salary and other income lost due to their reserve training and other duties associated with their military service. In addition, the Job Reservation Act requires employers to hold reservists' jobs for them, with all responsibilities and benefits, while they serve on active duty. Public sector employees typically continue to receive their salaries when on reserve training. Reservists also receive pension insurance, medical care, and unemployment insurance without charge from the *Bundeswehr*. Officers are reimbursed for outside costs related to their military duties.[119]

Although these benefits are generous, Germany's limited defense spending impedes the *Bundeswehr*'s ability to attract and keep voluntary reserve and regular personnel. The country spends approximately 1.4 percent of its gross domestic product (GDP) on defense, one of the lowest levels in NATO. Demographic trends, especially the overall aging of the German population and the declining number of births, suggest the current challenging situation will only worsen. Unless the German government is willing to spend considerably more on military affairs and public service functions performed by conscientious objectors, the country is likely to continue to rely on conscription.

CHAPTER 6

CANADA

The Canadian Forces (CF) consist of two components: the Regular Force and the Reserve Force. The Canadian Reserve Force itself has four main components: the Primary Reserve (P Res), the Supplementary Reserve (Sup Res), the Cadet Instructor Cadre (CIC), and the Canadian Rangers. Canadian reservists serve on a voluntary basis for an indefinite period. Although most combat and service support occupations exist in both the Regular and Reserve forces, the Canadian Department of Defence recently created reserve-specific classifications in order to take better advantage of reservists' civilian professional qualifications and experience.[120]

The government considers the P Res the preferred reserve component for most operations. It has contributed approximately 10 percent of the Canadian forces involved in recent foreign military operations.[121] Its members have responsibility for certain active-duty tasks not assigned to the Regular Forces. The P Res is further split into Service components.[122] The Army Reserve, called the Militia, is by far the largest of the P Res components. With 15,500 soldiers, the Militia serves several vital functions. Most importantly, it provides the Regular Army with the resources needed to augment the active-duty forces in an emergency and helps "connect" the Army with Canadian civilians. The Naval Reserve, commanded by the Chief of Maritime Staff, provides the crew for 10 of the Navy's 12 maritime coastal patrol vessels and performs coastal operations not assigned to the active-duty Navy. Such operations include port security, mine countermeasures, and intelligence functions relating to the Navy's control of shipping. In 2005-06, the total strength of the Naval Reserves stood at 4,000. The government intends to increase that number to 5,130 by 2015.

Unlike the previous two P Res components, the Air Reserve is fully integrated into the active-duty Air Force. There is no specific unit-level breakdown for the 2,600 strong Air Reserves. This integration is crucial because the regular Air Force has found it difficult to cope with the high operational demands of recent years. The Air Reserve provides more than a third of Air Force personnel assigned to "incremental" tasks. It also supplies 10 percent of Air Force personnel deployed on overseas operations. The Air Force has a formal policy of facilitating transfers between its Reserve and Regular components. In recent years, it has adopted measures to harmonize career policies that previously restricted movement between them.[123]

The remaining components of the P Res force are the Communication Reserve, the Health Services Reserve, and the Legal Reserve. The formation of the Communication Reserve Information Protection Team (CRIPT) has strengthened the role of reservists in this area. CRIPT aims to enhance Reserve support for the Canadian Forces Information Operations Group by providing information-protection services. The Health Services Reserve trains its 1,200 personnel to support and sustain CF Health Services Group Elements in operations. Its members also provide health services support to their assigned Canadian Brigade group and contribute to the Health Services Primary Reserve List. Members on the List engage in a variety of roles ranging from supporting clinics in Canada to deploying overseas. Finally, the Legal Reserve consists of qualified part-time lawyers serving in the military. Their careers closely resemble those of their regular counterparts.[124]

The second of the four components of the Reserve Forces is the Supplementary Reserve, which serves as a list of some 40,000 former CF members whom the government can easily recall to active duty. Members of the Sup Res can volunteer for limited duration full-time service in support of a specific operation. In this case, the member would be assigned to either the Regular Forces or the P Res, in effect upgrading his or her Reserve role. Sup Res forces are required to train and perform their duties only when they are activated.[125]

A third component of the Reserve forces is the Cadet Instructor Cadre (CIC). It supervises and trains the federally-sponsored Cadet program for teenagers between the ages of 12 and 18. This program seeks to develop "good citizenship and leadership, promoting physical fitness, and stimulating the interest of youth in the sea, land and air activities of the Canadian Forces."[126] In effect, CIC officers have responsibility for helping recruit and train the future generation of Canada's military forces.

The Canadian Rangers represent the final reserve component. Their main responsibility is to provide a military presence in Canada's sparsely settled and isolated northern and coastal areas. Their role is important in regions that cannot be covered by other CF elements due to financial or logistical limitations. They also serve as first responders in remote regions stricken by natural disasters. The Rangers currently have approximately 4,000 members organized into over 100 patrol units. The government aims to have 4,800 Rangers by March 2008.[127]

Besides distinguishing among the four components, Canadian authorities categorize military reserve service according to three broad classes. A reservist's class of service determines the individual's rate of pay and whether his other employment is full- or part-time. Reservists may participate in more than one class of service at various times throughout their military careers. Class "A" service is similar to casual or part-time work. It requires a commitment of at least 4 evenings and 1 weekend per month between September and May each year. Reservists in this class are paid a full-day rate for periods of more than 6 working hours. If they work less than that, they are paid a half-day rate. Training cannot exceed more than 12 consecutive days for Class A reservists. Their benefit package is comprehensive, but not as generous as those provided to the CF. Class "B" reservists sign an agreement to train and work for a time period of anywhere between 14 and 365 consecutive days. They are paid at normal Reserve rates. Their benefit package is similar to that of Class A reserves if they serve less than 180 days, while those with more than 180 days service receive additional benefits. Class "C" reservists are those who work in the Regular Forces for a period greater than 90 days. These reservists are governed by Regular Force terms of service and hence receive Regular Force pay and benefits. Class C service is only offered to reservists on specific operations.[128]

Reservists normally serve on a part-time basis, though they can volunteer for limited-duration full-time employment in the CF. Canada's Privy Council last issued a mandatory call-up of the Reserve Forces in 1939 following the onset of World War II. The Vice Chief of the Defence Staff's Force Structure Guidance, published in 2000, further outlines how the Reserve Force will expand in the event of full-scale mobilization. The reservists also contribute to meeting Canadian defense needs in cases short of major wars. According to a 1994 Defence White Paper, "the Reserves are a national institution and provide a vital link between the Canadian Forces and local communities. Their primary role will be the augmentation, sustainment, and support of deployed forces."[129]

In recent years, the Department of Defence has enhanced the role of reservists in managing domestic emergencies. The government has repeatedly mobilized reservists for these purposes. In 1998, for instance, reservists helped localities recover from a devastating ice storm and assisted the authorities with the Swiss Air Flight 111 recovery operation. Canada also placed thousands of reservists on-call to manage anticipated disruptions from the Y-2K computer date rollover during the millennial transition. The Canadian Rangers regularly assist remote communities to recover from disasters such as plane crashes and avalanches. The 9/11 attacks and other terrorist incidents in North America have led the government to enhance the role of the reserve components in averting and responding to terrorist attacks on Canadian territory.

In accordance with a recommendation of a 1987 White Paper, Canada adopted a "Total Force" principle to govern the integration of its active and reserve components. Under this policy, Canada's reservists formally became an "integral part of Canada's defence structure on an equal footing with the Regular Forces."[130] As part of the Total Force concept, members of the P Res are required to meet the same standards as those of the Regular Force. Reservists selected for service on operations undertake mission-specific pre-deployment training. This training occurs in conjunction with that of any Regular Force personnel taking part in that mission, thus promoting active-reserve integration.

Several factors prompted the decision to adopt the Total Force policy. First, supporters of the concept wanted to save money by substituting less-expensive reserve forces for more costly active-duty troops. Second, they thought improved active-reserve integration would enhance the military effectiveness of Canada's defense forces. In the 1970s and 1980s, many reservists lacked specific wartime tasks and suffered from inadequate equipment and training. Finally, Canadian officials suspected they had failed to exploit the full potential of their reserve components. While most NATO countries had more soldiers in their reserve components than on active duty, the *Defence White Paper* lamented that Canada's Regular Force was four times larger than its Reserve Force.[131]

Canadian Reserve Forces have various multinational training opportunities with other NATO members. The Canadian Directorate of Reserves has the authority to sponsor up to six Primary Reservists to participate in the two exercises that NATO conducts in most years. The International Junior Officer Leadership Development Seminar (IJOLDS), open to any reserve junior officer with a rank higher than Second Lieutenant, allows officers to "come together for the purposes of sharing the common cultural values of reservists, building teamwork within international forces and expanding the personal and professional horizons of participants." Canadian reservists also can participate in the U.S. Reserve Components National Security Course (USRCNSC), which is open to senior primary reserve officers with the rank of Lieutenant Colonel or above.[132]

Within Canada, the military organizes three different Reserve training courses. First, the Advanced Logistics Officers Course (ALOC), open to P Res officers with certain qualifications (rank of major or lieutenant commander, 1-month availability, etc.), is offered twice a year. It "enhances the skills of personnel and enable[s] them to be employed in command and staff appointments by broadening their professional knowledge in the theory and practical application of logistics, resource management, and leadership." Second, the National Security Studies Seminar (NSSS) gives six senior reserve officers an opportunity to discuss theories and processes concerning national and international affairs. Finally, the Lester B. Pearson Canadian International Peacekeeping Training Center helps improve the performance of Canadian reservists when they deploy on humanitarian missions and post-conflict stability operations.[133] The Department of Defence tries to give all reservists who deploy to an operational theater at least 1 month of pre-deployment training.

Despite the long history of collaboration between the Canadian and U.S. militaries, it was not until 1999 that the two defense communities began to discuss reserve-specific issues on a regular basis. In that year, the two countries initiated annual summits of reserve officers. Their progress was most visible in addressing issues relating to information sharing as well as individual and unit exchanges. For example, the U.S. Army Civil Affairs and Psychological Operations Command (USACAPOC) helped Canadians develop their own capabilities in this area. Furthermore, the Canadian Land Force Reserve Restructure (LFRR) project has benefited from lessons and insights shared at these meetings. Personnel and unit exchanges have also been carried out under the forum's umbrella. Canada and the United States currently trade instructors for military education courses. They also exchange students in the Joint Reserve Command and Staff College and the Command and General Staff Officers Course. Finally, both reserve communities have expressed interest in creating a Reserve Officer Exchange Program similar to those which already exist between the United States and Germany, the United States and the United Kingdom, and between Canada and the United Kingdom.[134] Unfortunately, the events of 9/11, though highlighting the need for enhanced bilateral collaboration on homeland security issues, diverted attention from these initiatives. The military reserve leaders of both countries have instead focused attention on the large number of Canadian and U.S. reservists serving on active missions in Afghanistan, Iraq, and elsewhere. On a more positive note, these joint operations have enhanced mutual understanding and dialogue between the American and Canadian reserve communities regarding various operational issues.[135]

The "Total Force" policy has not achieved all its goals. The most comprehensive analysis of Canada's reserve components was the 2000 Fraser Report, formally entitled, *In Service of the Nation: Canada's Citizen Soldiers for the 21st Century*. In the report, John A. Fraser, the Chairman of a special committee charged with assessing the state of the country's reserve components and policies, highlighted continued problems in the training of Army reservists. In particular, the committee found that, although the Army leadership had tried to create "reserve-friendly" training packages, part-time soldiers could rarely achieve the same standards as full-time professionals. The Fraser Report offered a series of recommendations regarding how to deal with the training and other problems affecting the reserves. These included shortening and simplifying the enrollment process, granting local reserve units more leeway to design recruiting campaigns and schedule training sessions optimized to their regions' needs, and creating alternative terms of service to attract more volunteers.[136]

Since the publication of the Fraser Report, the Defence Department has undertaken several projects to overcome the substantial personnel shortfalls that persist within all elements of the Primary Reserve component. First, the CF Pension Modernization Project modified military pensions to reflect the increased demands placed on reservists under the Total Force concept. Starting in 2006, Primary Reservists can participate in a new pension arrangement that is based on their full-time or part-time military employment rather than whether they belong to the Regular or Reserve forces. Second, the Reserve Force Employment Project is reexamining the use of reservists in military missions given the continuing changes in the operational demands on the Regular forces. Third, the Reinstatement in Civil Employment Project has resulted in draft legislation to protect a reservist's employment during compulsory call-ups, which occur more often under the Total Force concept.[137] Canadian law lacks specific provisions that protect the civilian jobs of reservists—a practice at variance with that found in most of the other countries profiled. The government relies instead on a voluntary program that encourages civilian employers and other institutions to support reservists by providing either paid or unpaid leave for Reserve Force Members who need to undertake required training or military duties.[138]

Perhaps the most important enhancement program is the LFRR project. Since its implementation in October 2000, the initiative has sought to increase the strength of the Land Reserve and sustain it at this higher level. The LFRR Strategic Plan has two phases. Phase One, completed in FY 2003, "stabilized" the Army Reserve's organization and structure. The second phase, now nearly complete, seeks to increase the size of the force to 18,500 part-time soldiers from the Phase One total of 15,500. Phase Two also seeks to give reservists a better quality of life by improving their benefits, administration, training, and support.[139]

On April 15, 2005, the Canadian government released a major International Policy Statement (ISP) that discussed how Canadian foreign and defense policy would change to address the main challenges of the post-Cold War world.[140] In the area of defense, the document stated that the government would allocate 13 billion Canadian dollars for the country's armed forces during the next 5 years. The government plans to use the additional funds to increase the size of Canada's reserve forces by 3,000 people (and the regular forces by 5,000 personnel). The ISP will also allow the government to complete implementation of Phase II of the Land Force Reserve Restructure Program (including the Medical and Communications Reserves) and the raising of the force's authorized end-state to 18,500 personnel.

In addition, the ISP will allow the government to create additional specialized units in the reserve force. For example, the Land Forces (army) plans to build on the mix of military and civilian skills resident in the Reserves (e.g., chemical, biological, radiological and nuclear response, information operations and civil military cooperation), as well as their presence nationwide, to improve military support to civilian authorities responding to domestic emergencies. The armed forces plan to establish similar specialized capabilities and additional responsibilities in the maritime and air force reserve units. Finally, the government plans to augment the Canadian Rangers to enhance Canadian sovereignty and security in the north.

CHAPTER 7

AUSTRALIA

Until recently, Australians saw their reserve components as primarily a homeland defense force. Originally called the Citizen Military Forces (CMF), the reserves were primarily local militias designed to defend Australian territory in the unlikely event of foreign invasion. The Defence Act of 1903 explicitly prohibited the Army from using the CMF in foreign military operations. To circumvent that restriction in past wars, Australia has had to require compulsory military service and enact emergency legislative exemptions on the use of reservists. After World War II, the Australian Defence Force (ADF) tried to reduce its reliance on its reserve components. The Defence Act of 1974 changed the name of the CMF to the Army Reserves to emphasize its "secondary support position."[141]

The end of the Cold War, the rise of global terrorism, and Australia's increased foreign military engagements — the country's armed forces, including their reserve components, are cooperating more closely with their foreign counterparts in multilateral military operations than at any time in their history — have led the government to rethink this policy.[142] Australian policymakers concluded they no longer needed reserve components designed chiefly to provide the basis for expanding the ADF into a force for waging a protracted continental-scale military campaign. A 2001 amendment to the National Defence Act allowed the government to employ reservists in foreign operations ranging from disaster relief and humanitarian missions to major military campaigns. Since then, ADF reservists have deployed in operations throughout the world, including in Iraq, Afghanistan, East Timor, Sudan, and the Solomon Islands. Currently, over 2,000 ADF reservists are deployed on international military operations.[143]

At home, Australia's reservists have provided security at major events such as the 2000 Sydney Olympic Games, the Commonwealth Heads of Government Meeting, and the 2003 Rugby World Cup.[144] In late 2003, the Australian Army created its first antiterrorist unit, the Reserve Response Force (RRF), consisting solely of reservists. Its 1,000 members help guard both major events and Australia's critical infrastructure.[145] A 2005 *Defence Update* indicated that the government had directed the ADF to develop Active Reservists "with specific roles and tasks to support Australia's domestic security effort."[146]

According to The International Institute for Strategic Studies, the ADF currently has a total reserve force of 18,973 — with 15,000 members in the Army, 1,973 in the Navy, and 2,000 in the Air Force.[147] Those seeking to join their ranks must be Australian citizens or permanent residents seeking citizenship.[148] The minimum length of service varies depending on a reservist's rank, skill level, and military branch. Nontechnical applicants join the military for 4 years, while General Entry technical applicants have a 6-year commitment. Officers have more flexibility; their contracts typically range from 3 to 9 years, though Air Force pilots must join for 12 years.[149] Almost all (97 percent) reserve positions are available to women.[150] The ADF has created the Australian Defense Force Cadets (ADFC) as an umbrella organization for the three Service Cadet programs. The ADFC is open to young people 12 1/2 to 18 years old. It seeks to encourage youth participants to pursue military service through educational awards and opportunities for accelerated promotion.[151]

Australia has six categories of reservists: (1) High Readiness Reserves (whose members undergo additional training and service obligations); (2) High Readiness Specialist Reserves (who possess skills of high value to the military); (3) Specialist Reserves; (4) Active Reserves; (5) Standby Reserves; and (6) other categories determined by each individual branch. Most reservists fall into the fourth or fifth category. Members of the Active Reserve are primarily designed to supplement active-duty units, either through initial force allocation or through reinforcement of deployed forces. Legislation enacted in 2001, however, allows for their use in any national emergency. Standby Reserves are former members of the Regular Forces who do not have a training commitment. Like members of the Active Reserves, they are integrated into regular military operations when mobilized, but they are only called up during threats to national security or for major foreign missions.

The government also recognizes four types of reserve service: ordinary service, voluntary unprotected full-time service (who do not enjoy special job protection), voluntary protected full-time service, and compulsory full-time service (requiring a government call up). Regardless of category, all reserves must be available for "continuous full-time service" in a major war. Most mobilizations, however, occur in order to address national emergencies, help peacekeeping and disaster relief operations, provide military support to civilian authorities, or assist "significant national or international activities."[152]

Each branch of the military has unique training and service requirements for its reserve component. The

Navy requires a minimum of 20 days of training a year. Its reservists can serve on active duty for up to 100 days annually. Army Reservists usually train 1 night a week, 2 weeks a year, and 1 weekend a month. The Air Force Reserve requires a minimum of 32 training days per year, but some specializations demand as many as 60 days. Air Force Reservists can serve on active duty as many as 130 days annually. In all branches, additional training may be required for promotions.[153]

The Australian Army, like most Western militaries, has since the 1990s relied increasingly on its reservists to save money and supplement its overstretched active-duty units. It increased the size of its reserve component by almost 4,000 people, while reducing the number of regular troops by over 10,000.[154] When ADF units deployed to East Timor from 1999 to 2003, more Army Reservists were employed in full-time service than in all the years from 1945 to 1999.[155] Smaller numbers of Active Reservists have served in Rwanda (1994-95) and in Iraq (since 2003). Reservists are especially heavily involved in the Defence Health Services. For example, the majority of Australian personnel sent to assist nations devastated by the 2004 Asian Tsunami were reservists.[156]

The Army is undertaking a major restructuring of the Army Reserves (ARes) as part of the Hardened and Networked Arm (HNA) plan, whose implementation is scheduled to last until 2015. The objective is to improve reservists' direct support of Army operational units.[157] The need to respond rapidly to unexpected terrorist attacks and other emergencies also prompted the Army to create the new category of High Readiness Reserves. Their members commit to maintain elevated readiness and serve a minimum of 2 years. The Army organized these soldiers into small teams rather than larger units in order to mobilize these reservists more rapidly than in the past (within 30 days). Current plans are to increase their number to approximately 3,000.[158] Furthermore, the Army is also clarifying the chain of command for its reserve components and specifying how they will integrate with the Regular Army during call-ups.[159] The Army also is seeking to improve its reserve training programs, with a new Active Reserve Training Model designed to enable ARes members to develop narrow but thorough skills in important fields.[160]

The Naval Reserve (NR) historically existed to augment the Permanent Naval Force. During World War II, the Navy Reserves outnumbered the regular Navy four to one.[161] In 1990, the Royal Australian Navy (RAN) decided to integrate completely its reserve and active components as part of the RAN's total force concept.[162] Of the current NR components, Active Reservists work part time in the RAN, while Standby Reservists, though not generally obliged to work with the Navy, nevertheless are available to do so occasionally. The NR is an integral part of the Navy's management structure, with Active Reservists under Navy administrators and Standby Reservists under divisional officers, called Regional Reserve Pool Managers. The NR offers reservists billets both within predominately reserve units (such as diving teams or bands) and positions that involve routine interaction with the Regular Navy (such as Medical Officers and Seamen).[163]

As in the Army Reserve or the Naval Reserve, Royal Australian Air Force (RAAF) members on Standby Reserve must have prior military service. In addition, Active Reserve members wishing to become part of an aircrew must also have active-duty experience due to the highly technical nature of these positions. Unlike the Army Reserve and Naval Reserve, the Air Force Reserve has additional branches for those wishing to fulfill nontechnical and nonflying duties. The Contingency Operations Reserve Group (CORG) deploys nonflying support personnel to combat zones. Their annual training commitment is 32 days each year. The Ground Defence Reserve Group (GrDefRG), which requires a minimum of 50 days training per year, provides dedicated ground forces for Air Force units. Finally, the Operational Aircrew Reserve Group (OARG) consists of former active-duty aircrews who maintain a high degree of readiness to support Air Force flying missions. While the OARG only requires 32 training days per year, many of its members undergo additional training to maintain their flying skills.[164] The RAAF also established a High Readiness Reserve (HRR) unit to provide personnel who can deploy rapidly to distant theaters. They receive specialized training to enhance their integration into regular RAAF units.

Over the years, the government has taken steps to improve reservists' relations with their employers. Despite continued complaints, public law until recently did not protect the jobs of reservists who volunteered for service. The Defence Reserve Service (Protection) Act of 2001 now requires employers to grant their employees leave for reserve training and outlaws discrimination against employees or prospective employees serving in the military.[165] The Act created a new Office of Reserve Service Protection to provide guidance about the Act's requirements to both reservists and their employers. It also investigates and resolves disputes arising from its provisions, provides extra help to self-employed reservists, and seeks generally to enhance reservists' availability for military service.[166] Each type of state protection for reservists — discrimination, employment, partnership, education, financial liability, and loans and guarantees — applies to a certain range of reserve service. For example, protection against discrimination applies to all types of reserve service, while only mobilized reservists receive bankruptcy protection.[167] Since 2003, the government has required the Australian Public Service to include provisions for reserve leave in its job contracts.[168]

The 2001 Protection Act also guaranteed employers that reservists would return to work as soon as their service terms ended. In addition, the government agreed to compensate employers for any losses resulting from their employees' reserve service. The Employer Support Payment Scheme (ESP), introduced in June 2005, offsets the cost of employees engaged in most categories of ADF service. Its weekly compensation rate is equivalent to the average weekly earnings of a full-time adult Australian worker. The ESP encompasses full-time, part-time, and self-employed workers that meet certain conditions.[169] The government also provides employers with a weekly payment of about $1,000 AU (U.S. $750) for each employee who is absent performing military service. Employers of health professionals can receive as much as $5,600 AU (U.S. $4,200) per week per released reservist.[170] The Defence Reserves Support Council (DRSC) has committees in each state and territory that educate employers about their reservists' service and reward excellence in civilian and military work.[171] The individual military services have taken additional steps to make reserve duty more palatable for employers. The training requirements for the Air Force Reserve are considered especially onerous and can often interfere with civilian employment. To ease this burden, the Air Force has expanded its training facilities so that the required courses can be completed locally. It has also reduced the number of specialized training classes that must be taken off-site.[172]

These initiatives appear to have achieved some success. In a 2004 survey, only one-fifth of the reservists employed in the civilian workforce reported difficulty obtaining permission to participate in reserve activities during workdays.[173] Nevertheless, the ADF reserve components continue to experience major recruitment shortfalls. During the 2003-04 recruiting period, the overall ADF reserve force achieved only 80 percent of its recruiting target, with the Navy Reserve reaching 42 percent, the Army Reserve 84 percent, and the Air Force Reserve 52 percent. This represented a drop from the 85 percentage achieved by the reserve force overall in the 2002-03 period.[174] The shrinking reserve force has become a matter of great concern for Australian defense analysts. From 1995-2005, the Active Reserve decreased by 24 percent. The Army Reserve, which decreased from 24,500 in 1995 to 17,000 in 2004, has been most seriously affected.[175] (The RAAF Reserve actually grew from 1,500 in 1995 to 2,500 in 2005.) Widespread absenteeism within the reserve components compounds this problem. Between 1999 and 2003, over 20 percent of reservists failed to report for duty.[176]

Several explanations could explain the declining number of reservists. The Army's new centralized and privatized system of recruitment, for instance, has proved less successful than the prior system relying primarily on regional reserve units to recruit their members. Another factor may have been the lengthening in the initial training period for reservists, which recently increased from 2 to 6 weeks.

Demographics may also play a role. Australia's 18-25 year-old population is now smaller than at any time since World War II. Finally, more positive factors may be at work, including the country's low unemployment and vibrant economy as well as the voluntary entry of many Army Reserve members into the Regular Army.[177]

To increase the attractiveness of reserve military service, the Kokoda Foundation, an Australian military think tank, has proposed a National Security Education Initiative whereby the government would fund university studies for students who would commit to serve in the reserves after graduating.[178] The government has thus far declined to implement such an initiative. Instead, it has pledged to spend more over the next decade on remunerating Active and High Readiness Reserves through additional allowances, improved health benefits, and annual completion bonuses. It also will hire more civilian contactors to perform nonoperational missions (e.g., logistics) traditionally undertaken by reservists.[179] Arguing that Australia's reserve components contribute little to the ADF's operational potential despite receiving about $1 billion AU ($750 million) annually, critics favor spending more on regular forces.[180]

The Australian government has pledged to spend more over the next decade on remunerating Active and High Readiness Reserves through higher salaries, improved health benefits, paid public sector leave policies, annual completion bonuses, and a new "Academic Support Policy" for Reservists undertaking post-secondary education at Australian universities and colleges.[181] It also will hire more civilian contractors to perform non-operational missions (e.g., logistics) traditionally undertaken by reservists.[182] Critics who favor spending more on regular forces argue that Australia's reserves contribute little to the ADF's operational potential despite receiving $1 billion AU ($750 million) annually.[183]

CHAPTER 8

CHINA

In recent years, China's extraordinary economic growth has enabled the government to transform its military, the People's Liberation Army (*zhongguo renmin jiefangjun;* or PLA), into a potent armed force. This year's annual U.S. Defense Department report on Chinese military power highlights that the PLA is in the process of transitioning "from a mass army designed for protracted wars of attrition on its territory to a more modern force capable of fighting short duration, high intensity conflicts against high-tech adversaries."[184] As Chinese military doctrine has evolved from "people's war" to "limited war under high-technology conditions" to the new concept of network-centric operations, the PLA has been developing its reserve components to help provide the capabilities required for the new missions.

During the past 2 decades, Chinese leaders have sought to develop "a crack regular force with strong reserve strength."[185] Like other great powers, China has increased reliance on its reserve components (*yubeiyi budui*) as it has reduced the size of its active-duty (*xianyi budui*) forces. Although the PLA remains the largest military in the world, consisting of both short-term conscripts and long-term professionals, over the last 2 decades China has downsized its regular forces by millions of people. Furthermore, the Chinese Army, Navy, and Air Force shortened their conscription terms from 3 or 4 years to 2 years in 1999. Through these reductions, the PLA seeks to field a smaller number of better motivated and equipped active and reserve units capable of waging limited wars and combined arms operations under modern conditions.[186]

The PLA's reserve components, reestablished in 1983, remain closely tied to their active-duty counterparts. The original function of the reserves was to supplement the regular Army in the protracted conventional conflict of attrition envisaged by Chinese military doctrine — either on Chinese territory or in adjacent regions (e.g., a renewed war in Korea or Vietnam).[187] As the PLA's capabilities grew in sophistication during the 1990s, its original land reserve component matured into separate components for the Army, Navy, Air Force, and Second Artillery Force (in charge of China's nuclear forces ballistic missile arsenal).[188] The Central Military Commission (CMC) testified to the reserve's growing importance in 1996 when it decided to confer military ranks on reserve officers.[189] In April 1998, the CMC ordered the leaders of the country's military districts to expand the reserve units in their jurisdictions.[190] At the end of 1998, the government amended China's Military Service Law to improve the status of older reservists, aged 29-35, who could contribute desirable skills to the country's increasingly high-tech military. In 2002, the CMC launched an initiative to improve the effectiveness of the reserve units in China's cities.

Today, China's numerous reserve units — organized into divisions, brigades, and regiments — are incorporated directly into the PLA's order of battle. The PLA currently has an estimated 500,000 to 800,000 reservists organized into some 30 infantry divisions, 12 air defense divisions, and seven logistics support brigades.[191] A reserve infantry division, the largest PLA reserve unit, contains more than 10,000 officers and troops. Every Military Region now has a reserve logistics brigade to support reserve and active-duty operations in the area. Their missions include assisting with military maintenance, repair, transportation, communications, and command and control.[192] All reserve units have a small cadre of active-duty personnel. They presumably administer the formation's affairs between mobilizations and serve as a nucleus for reconstituting the unit during call-ups. Besides reserve units operating as separate entities, either independently or as components of larger formations, the PLA Navy (PLAN), PLA Air Force (PLAAF), and Second Artillery Force have assigned some reservists to provide individual replacements for vacancies that arise in active-duty units.[193]

The Chinese Military Service Law specifies that all male citizens between the ages of 18 and 22 are liable for compulsory active-duty service. Many Chinese not conscripted have historically joined the People's Militia or People's Armed Police (PAP).[194] Reservists remain predominantly former regular soldiers and officers who have been discharged from active duty, but not all demobilized PLA regulars join the reserves. In recent years, moreover, reserve units have increasingly included civilians who, because of various legal draft exemptions, lack prior military experience yet possess specialized technical skills of military value. Similarly, a number of reserve officers are graduates of the reserve officers training programs recently established in China's major civilian universities and high schools.[195] Reserve officers are typically classified as either Category I full-time reservists or Category II part-time reservists. Category I reserve officers normally serve as military commanders of company or higher-level units, while Category II reservists usually function as political commissars or technical specialists.[196] When they reach the age limit of their Military Service, reservists are expected to retire or join the People's Militia.

A nationwide network of Defense Mobilization Committees — which integrate military, government, and Communist Party leaders at all levels of government — manages all reserve activation issues, including training and equipping reservists, administering their call-ups, and transporting them to their place of operation.[197] The committees could serve as the nucleus of joint military-civilian headquarters in times of war or crisis.[198] Each reserve unit falls under the dual authority of both the PLA hierarchy and the regional Party and government organs. In peacetime, the Army reserve is subordinate to the provincial or municipal commands, while the reserve units of the PLAN, PLAAF, and Second Artillery come under the joint control of both the provincial commands and the branch commands of the relevant Service. Upon mobilization in wartime, they follow the leadership of the commander of their designated active-duty unit.[199]

To enable reservists to fulfill their expanding military responsibilities, the government has increased the money and time spent on their training and equipment. Reserve units now train directly with active-duty PLA forces, using both traditional on-base training and more advanced simulation and network training.[200] As in other countries, the PLA has traditionally exploited the civilian skills of its members. For example, reservists working in the civilian chemical industry serve in chemical warfare units. China's economic transformation has been creating new high-technology sectors in the civilian economy, especially in the area of information technology. These developments provide a basis for generating new reserve units (including high-readiness "fist" units) that can apply these advanced civilian skills to the military sector. For instance, during the past decade, the PLA has created reserve units specializing in advanced information warfare (IW) and information operations (IO) whose personnel consist largely of civilian telecommunications workers.[201] The U.S. DoD reports that civilian information technology (IT) experts in reserve and militia units regularly train and exercise together with active-duty forces.[202]

PLA reservists commonly participate in disaster relief, emergency rescue, and post-disaster reconstruction operations. Reservists with specialized expertise in the areas of medicine and engineering are especially valuable as supplementary first responders. During the severe flooding in 1998, several million reservists participated in relief efforts. More recently, the government has mobilized hundreds of thousands of reservists in response to epidemic diseases such as severe acute respiratory syndrome (SARS) and natural disasters such as forest fires and earthquakes. Reservists involved in these operations fall under the command of a joint military-civilian headquarters.[203] In the case of a domestic emergency, the authorities can also call up reservists to assist civilian law enforcement bodies with maintaining internal security. In responding to the mass demonstrations that have become increasingly common in China in recent years, however, the authorities have preferred to rely on the local police or other specialized internal security units rather than the PLA.[204]

The March 1997 Law on National Defense describes two components of the Chinese armed forces (*wuzhuang liliang*) as having more prominent internal security functions than the PLA. The first of these paramilitary components, the People's Militia (*renmin minbing*), still maintains large part-time units that could also function as a reserve manpower pool for the PLA during wartime. The Chinese Communist Party (CCP) and the PLA General Staff jointly supervise militia affairs. Each military area command is responsible for managing the militia in its jurisdiction.[205] In the 1940s and 1950s, the militia constituted a key element of the people's war doctrine, playing a significant role in the CCP's victory in the Chinese Civil War. During the 1960s and 1970s, the militia worked closely with the PLA regular forces to defend China's territory from attack.[206] In the 1990s, militia units provided labor at the Three Gorges Dam and other key construction projects. The two-million strong paramilitary Xinjiang Production and Construction Corps also operated farms and other business in Xinjiang Uighur Autonomous Region, while simultaneously maintaining security among the discontented ethnic Uighur population.[207] More recently, the size and role of the militia have declined as the PLA has become a more modern and mobile force focused on conflicts along China's periphery.[208]

At present, the People's Militia performs primarily rear area support. Its main responsibility is basic area defense, which in some regions can include protecting China's borders and critical infrastructure (e.g., transportation, communications, and energy networks). The militia includes both ordinary and "primary" members. The ordinary militia numbers in the tens of millions, but its units have minimal training and capabilities. The smaller primary militia has approximately 10 million members. They receive the bulk of the national government's attention, training, and funding. Members of the primary militia are typically younger than ordinary militia personnel and are more likely to have recently served on active duty. Primary militia formations include rapid reaction and specialized technical units. For example, the PLA trains and equips its special urban militia units to perform air defense and infrastructure repair in wartime.[209]

The People's Armed Police (PAP) (*zhongguo renmin wuzhuang jingcha budui*) represents the third component of the Chinese armed forces. Although conscripted through the same procedures as the PLA, the PAP employs an independent training and education program. Its approximately 1.5 million personnel fall under a military chain of command as well as the authority of the central Ministry of Public Security and the relevant local government authorities.[210] It has several types of paramilitary units (an Internal Guards Corps, Border Defense Corps, Forestry Corps, etc.) that differ in size, location, and mission.[211] Most units have internal security as a primary duty. All PAP forces receive some training in light infantry missions.[212] Some of the most capable PAP contingents had belonged to the PLA's regular forces before the 1990s. The PAP receives funding from both central and local government ministries, as well as from its own businesses, the fines it levies, and specific institutions that use its security services (e.g., protecting a government building).[213] In peacetime, its main functions encompass infrastructure protection, disaster relief, border control (including at inland ports and airports) and internal security—including countering terrorist attacks, controlling riots and other mass disturbances, and guarding Chinese prisons. The PAP also includes the State Guests Protection Unit, which provides security for senior officials.[214] In wartime, many PAP units probably would take on additional missions. These tasks could include assisting the PLA with local area defense and rear-area support missions such as traffic management and population control.[215]

CHAPTER 9

JAPAN

The Japanese Self-Defense Force (SDF) is currently in a state of flux. Seeking to manage the new threats of the 21st century and remain interoperable with the U.S. military, the SDF is becoming more agile and technologically advanced.[216] As part of this process, the SDF reserve components are undergoing a comprehensive transformation. During the Cold War, the United States assumed complete responsibility for defending Japan against external threats. Japanese decisionmakers did not anticipate mobilizing their military reserves except in a national emergency, most likely a full-scale invasion of the homeland. Since Japanese military planners considered this scenario implausible, they regularly underfunded, undertrained, and perhaps underutilized their reserve forces. Sporadic training, low compensation, and a weak officer cadre further relegated the SDF's reserve components to the periphery of the Japanese defense establishment.[217] During the last decade, however, the changing nature of both the general international security environment and the specific threats to Japan has led the government to restructure and reinvigorate the SDF reserve components.

Since Japan's frustrating experience during the 1991 Persian Gulf War when Tokyo's multi-billion dollar assistance package yielded only disparaging comments about "checkbook diplomacy," Japanese leaders have gradually expanded their involvement in international security issues. In June 1992, the Japanese Diet passed the International Peace Cooperation Law authorizing the SDF to participate in UN peacekeeping and international humanitarian relief operations under certain conditions.[218] The Japanese military subsequently contributed to noncombatant UN missions in Cambodia, Rwanda, East Timor, and other post-conflict regions.[219] Following Japan's uncertain response in 1994 to a U.S. request for assistance during a possible confrontation with North Korea over its nuclear weapons program, Tokyo and Washington in 1997 announced revisions to the Guidelines for U.S.-Japan Defense Cooperation. Among other things, the modifications specified that Japan would provide "rear area support" and "operational cooperation" (e.g., intelligence gathering, surveillance, and minesweeping) for American forces "in situations in areas surrounding Japan that will have an important influence on Japan's peace and security."[220]

The Anti-Terrorism Special Measures Law of October 2001, renewed in subsequent years, enabled the SDF to dispatch warships to the Indian Ocean to provide logistical support (primarily at-sea refueling) for allied military operations in Afghanistan as part of Operation ENDURING FREEDOM.[221] It marked the first SDF deployment in a theater of war. The Iraq Humanitarian Reconstruction Support Special Measures Law of July 2003 permitted the government to deploy ground troops in Iraq to provide logistical support for the allied military campaign there. The SDF contingent that served in Iraq from January 2004 until July 2006 represented the largest and most dangerous overseas Japanese military operation since World War II.

Besides describing China and North Korea as potential threats, Japan's December 2004 *National Defense Program Guidelines* stressed the need to improve the country's ability to conduct joint military operations with the United States in additional areas. In February 2005, the U.S.-Japan Security Consultative Committee (SCC) cited "the need to continue examining the roles, missions, and capabilities of Japan's Self Defense Forces and the U.S. Armed Forces required to respond effectively to diverse challenges in a well-coordinated manner."[222] A few months later, Japanese forces participated for the first time in the COBRA GOLD military exercise with the United States, Thailand, and Singapore.[223] With 240,000 troops, extensive air and naval power, and a $50-billion annual budget, the SDF could provide key assistance to an overtaxed U.S. military in certain East Asian contingencies.[224]

The ruling Liberal Democratic Party has been pushing to modify the traditional Japanese interpretation of their post-war constitution, especially Article 9's perceived restrictions on Japan's contribution to collective self-defense activities, to allow the SDF to play a greater role in improving the international security environment.[225] Amending the constitution would require a two-thirds majority vote in both houses of the Diet, as well as an affirmative majority in a subsequent national referendum. Although this political process could take years, Japan's external security role will likely continue to expand on a less formal basis as long as the public continues to feel threatened. Alarm over menacing North Korean behavior initially motivated many of the changes in Japan's regional security policies, but growing concern over China has substantially lessened traditional public apprehensions about expanding the SDF's roles and capabilities.[226] A December 2005 public opinion poll conducted by the *Nikkei Shimbun* found that 69 percent of respondents said people "cannot trust" China, compared with only

14 percent who said China could be trusted. Only 35 percent of the 904 people polled said they could not trust the United States.[227]

Although the Japanese continue to see China as replete with commercial opportunities, recent Chinese actions have alarmed Japan's leaders and public alike. During the 1996 Taiwan Strait Crisis, China launched missiles in the island's vicinity, threatening regional maritime commerce. Some of the missiles landed less than 100 kilometers from Okinawa.[228] Only a few months later, the sovereignty dispute between China and Japan over the Senkaku/Diaoyutai Islands revived. Since the late 1990s, Chinese ships have conducted unauthorized "research" within waters claimed by Japan, exacerbating their bilateral dispute over exploratory drilling rights in undersea natural gas fields in the East China Sea. In November 2004, the Japanese detected a Chinese nuclear submarine in their territorial waters. The government publication *Defense of Japan 2005* identified China's military modernization as potentially threatening and called on Beijing to make its defense programs more transparent.[229]

Japan's *National Defense Program Guidelines* for fiscal year 2005 reaffirmed the traditional SDF role of defending against invasions of Japan's offshore islands and intrusions into Japanese airspace and territorial waters. The Guidelines also recommended that the SDF improve its ability to respond to new threats such as attacks involving ballistic missiles, guerrillas and special operations forces. Furthermore, they called for enhancing the SDF's capacity to forestall possible disasters involving nuclear, biological, chemical, and radiological materials.[230] To respond to these new challenges, the SDF has been seeking to substitute quality for quantity throughout its ranks, especially in the reserves. For example, the government has raised entry standards for new reserve recruits to attract fewer inexperienced reservists and more SDF veterans.

The SDF consists of a ground, maritime, and air service. The Ground Self-Defense Force (GSDF) is the largest of the three services, totaling some 148,300 personnel in early 2007. The Maritime Self-Defense Force (MSDF) currently numbers 44,500 personnel. The Air Self-Defense Force (ASDF) has approximately 45,900 troops. The Central Staff amounts to 1,700 personnel. The combined strength of the SDF reserve components amounts to 41,800 — 33,800 in the GSDF Ready Reserve, 1,000 in the Navy Reserve, and 800 in the Air Reserve.[231] In order to differentiate among reservists with varying functions, skills, and experience levels, the Japan Defense Agency (JDA) breaks down Japanese reserve components into three categories: Regular Reserves (normally called "Reserve Personnel"), High-Readiness Reserves (normally "Ready Reserve Personnel"), and Reserve Candidates (normally "Candidates for SDF Reserve Personnel").[232]

Regular Reserves are part-time SDF personnel — normally engaged in full-time employment or study — that perform mainly administrative, logistical, and other support functions. In times of war or emergency, they can substitute for active-duty units engaged in front-line operations by assuming responsibility for rear-area security and logistical support. Regular Reserves volunteer for a renewable 3-year term of service and normally train only 5 days each year. Its members typically have at least 1 year of active duty experience or have graduated from "candidate" status.

High-Readiness Reserves consist of selected Regular Reserves in GSDF and recently retired GSDF members who agree to rejoin pre-designated GSDF units during an emergency. High-Readiness Reserves report for 30 days of training annually for a minimum of 3 years. Since they receive more extensive training than Regular Reserves, the JDA considers them most qualified to join front-line active-duty units in combat operations as well as in homeland security missions. The latter can include responding to both natural disasters and accidents (e.g., at one of Japan's civilian nuclear power facilities).[233] Training programs for High-Readiness Reserves are held on a number of separate occasions throughout the year to accommodate reservists' civilian schedules.

The JDA created the category of Reserve Candidates in 2001. The aim was to broaden the range of potential military recruits, increase contacts between the Japanese military and society, and enhance the SDF's access to utilize professional and technical skills found primarily in the civilian economy.[234] Reserve Candidates are not required to have served as regular SDF personnel, and few have prior military experience. They are also not liable to mobilization orders—only training call-ups. The SDF divides Reserve Candidates into two sub-categories: general and technical candidates. General candidates perform support functions such as rear-area security. After 50 days of training over the course of 3 years, they graduate into the Regular Reserves, with the same rights and duties as other members. Technical candidates fill specialized positions such as medical personnel, language experts, computer experts, architects, and vehicle maintenance personnel. After the successful completion of 10 days of training in 2 years, the technical candidates advance into the Regular Reserves.

The salary for each category of reserves differs substantially. Regular Reserves receive 88,500 yen

(U.S. $750) each year, consisting of 8,100 yen ($70) for each day of service and an additional 4,000 ($34) yen monthly allowance. Reserve Candidates receive 7,900 yen ($67) per day of education as well as allowances for training call-ups. Compensation for High-Readiness Reserves depends on the ranks and experience of each individual soldier. On average, a High-Readiness reservist receives approximately 600,000 yen ($5,100) annually in personnel allowances, training call-up allowances, and a continuous service incentive for those who satisfactorily complete their 3-year service commitment.[235]

These monetary incentives have proved most attractive to Reserve Candidates. Since people with no prior military experience can become Reserve Candidates, university students often join to supplement their incomes. In contrast, Japanese recruiters have found it more difficult to attract High-Readiness Reserves. One reason is that Japanese companies, facing shortages of skilled labor, discourage experienced former soldiers from committing to 30 days of annual training in the reserves. Although the government now offers an annual subsidy of 500,000 yen ($4,250) per person to employers of active High-Readiness reservists, JDA officials still complain that private employers discourage their best employees from entering the military. A Japanese executive reportedly told a JDA official that, "We must protect our company before we protect the nation."[236] Lingering anti-militarism also diminishes the attractiveness of reserve or other military service. Conversely, so does the lack of opportunities for operational experience for those Japanese desiring to participate in either peacekeeping missions or in combat scenarios. Until now, the SDF has never called up its reserve components except for training purposes.

The transformation of the SDF's reserve components could facilitate Japanese participation in U.S.-led security missions in the Asia-Pacific region. In particular, reservists could apply their civilian skills to joint post-conflict reconstruction operations and humanitarian missions such as the December 2004 Asian Tsunami relief and recovery effort. Surveys show overwhelming public support for SDF participation in disaster-relief activities both within Japan and overseas.[237] SDF reservists could apply many of the skills they develop for responding to natural disasters toward managing the consequences of terrorist attacks or human-made accidents. Japanese reservists could also support maritime security and missile defense missions in the regions surrounding Japan. Even though their engagement in actual combat operations is unlikely, their involvement would free up American troops for other roles.[238] To make such operations more effective, however, U.S. and Japanese defense planners should expand the involvement of their reserve components in joint military exercises and bilateral dialogue on potential East Asian security contingencies. Establishing additional mechanisms to exchange information on reserve issues — including lessons learned, best practices, and future transformation plans — could also prove profitable.

CHAPTER 10

ISRAEL

Israel's military reserve system provides an indispensable base for sustaining the conscript and professional superstructure of the Israeli Defense Forces (IDF). Since Israelis have historically found themselves surrounded by potentially hostile countries with much larger populations, they have designed a framework for quickly mobilizing large numbers of battle-ready forces in an emergency. As a result, Israeli planners have traditionally treated reservists as core combat troops—essential for any major operation—rather than as supplementary forces.[239] Israel requires almost all active duty personnel to transfer to the reserves after completing their regular service. The government allocates considerable funds to educate, train, and equip reservists (especially reserve officers) in order to maintain them at a high state of readiness. It also invests heavily in intelligence assets designed to provide the military with the advanced warning required to mobilize reservists rapidly in an emergency.

Israel's military and civilian sectors overlap considerably more than those of most countries. Large numbers of conscripts and reservists continually cycle through the IDF's active-duty components. These IDF regular forces consist of professional officers, noncommissioned officers, volunteer soldiers, and conscripts. The system of compulsory military service obligates both male and female citizens, 18 years or older, to serve on active duty in the IDF. Male officers must serve in the regular army for 48 months, male nonofficers for 36 months, and females for 24 months. The main groups exempted from universal conscription include male students of yeshiva religious schools (who may defer entry as long as their studies continue); religious females who choose to pursue alternative national service; women who marry or have children; members of most religious minorities (Druze are liable for military service; Christians and Muslims may volunteer to serve); and those deemed physically or psychologically unfit.

The members of Israel's regular army (*Sherut Qivah*) number far fewer than the reservists (*Zahal*). Over the past 25 years, the reserve components have accounted for approximately 75 percent of Israel's total military manpower.[240] Regular IDF members have varying terms of active-duty service. Specialists (e.g., pilots) typically must commit to multiyear contracts in return for expensive government-funded training. The IDF encourages most officers to pursue a civilian career after the completion of military service. This practice promotes a high rate of turnover in IDF leadership ranks while keeping the military closely tied to the civilian world. Israelis also believe that universal military service helps integrate their large immigrant population.

Most Israelis enter the reserves immediately following a 2- or 3-year stint in the regular forces. Until recently, most male reservists had to undergo approximately 1 month of annual training until they reached the age of 40. Certain specialists and some former active-duty soldiers volunteer to serve in the reserves until age 60, though combat soldiers often transfer to logistical units when they reach age 35.[241] Female reservists are liable for periodic training until they attain the maximum age of 40, get married, or have children. In practice, however, the government rarely calls up female reservists except for specialists in military intelligence or other key fields.[242] Non-Jews who serve in the regular forces are also liable for reserve duty.

The Israeli military keeps the precise number of its reserve and regular soldiers classified. The International Institute for Strategic Studies estimates the IDF reserve components at 408,000, with some 24,500 assigned to the air forces and 3,500 to naval units.[243] (The IDF constitutes a single unified service with two semi-independent branches, the Israeli Air Force and the Israeli Navy). The Institute for Advanced Strategic and Political Studies estimates that Israel's reserve components have a natural annual growth rate of 3 percent due to such factors as immigration and birth rates.[244] In recent years, however, the IDF has sought to reduce its reliance on reservists in combat situations and decrease the overall number of reservists.

The Israeli government developed its mass mobilization framework soon after the country's 1948-49 War of Independence, when the army took months to reach full strength. After visiting Switzerland, General Yigael Yadin, IDF Chief of Staff from 1949-1952, decided that Israel should develop a similar reserve system—modified to fit Israel's distinct circumstances.[245] On the one hand, Israel's economic condition precluded the possibility of maintaining a large standing army. On the other, the country's lack of strategic depth made it vulnerable to a surprise attack—ruling out the Soviet model of mobilizing enormous numbers of reservists over the course of weeks and months.

Given these imperatives, Israel constructed a unique system that relies on the rapid mobilization of large numbers of well-trained reservists to complement its smaller regular force. Most reservists are expected to join their units and acquire their equipment within 24-48 hours of receiving a call-up order. Some specialized units are required to mobilize even faster. The IDF expects Air Force reservists, for example, to respond within hours of a surprise attack. Their function is to begin attacking enemy forces immediately while also protecting less-ready IDF units undergoing mobilization. For this reason, IDF regulations require reserve pilots to fly a minimum number of hours each month to maintain their operational proficiency. If properly implemented, the present military reserve system should be capable of mobilizing hundreds of thousands of reservists within 2 days of a call-up.

For several years following Israel's independence, IDF reservists were organized into separate companies, battalions, and brigades distinct from active-duty units.[246] The decision to abandon this model proved advantageous in terms of both combat effectiveness and civil-military relations. Under the current system, reservists provide the IDF with a general source of trained personnel rather than constituting a separate branch of the military.[247] One distinct advantage to having such a large number of civilian reservists serving throughout the IDF is that their presence helps counter concerns about Israel's transformation into a militarized garrison state.[248]

To enhance unit cohesion, reservists have historically been assigned to military formations containing many of their former active-duty colleagues. Since reservists typically train at most for only 1 month each year, however, their weaponry skills frequently lag behind those of the regular forces. To reduce the impact of this gap, the IDF regularly combines regular and reserve forces in larger units. For example, many Air Force formations have a core group of conscript and professional personnel who, in an emergency, are reinforced by reservists. Reserve officers occupy leadership positions in all types of units.

During the early 1950s, reservists received training and equipment inferior to that of the regular forces. Following the 1956 Suez War, then IDF Chief of Staff Yitzhak Rabin implemented measures to improve reserve training and strengthen reservists' combat effectiveness. His initiatives helped transform the reserves from a ragtag militia into a highly capable force with an experienced officer corps and superior equipment.[249] Combined with Israel's preemptive approach to confronting external threats, the system of rapid mass mobilization contributed to Israel's overwhelming military victory in the Six Day War of 1967. The government's decision to delay mobilizing the reserves in advance of the Yom Kippur War of 1973 — due to economic and diplomatic concerns, as well as incorrect intelligence assessments — almost led to Israel's defeat during the early phases of that conflict.[250] After this experience, the IDF increased the size of its reserve components by, among other measures, making it harder for Israelis to avoid military service.[251]

General Yadin famously characterized the Israeli reservist as a "soldier on 11 months annual leave."[252] Although Israeli legislation imposes general limits on the number of days the government can call up soldiers and officers each year, various emergency laws have permitted reservists to serve for much longer periods during wars and other crises. After the 1967 war, for instance, reservists were stationed in the newly occupied Sinai Desert for several months at a time, a situation that led the IDF to introduce a rotation system.

The 1968 National Insurance Law established a unique system — a National Insurance Institute — to compensate reservists who must leave their workplace to perform their military duty. Before 1996, reservists' wages came entirely from insurance premiums collected from Israel's employers and salaried workers. Since then, the Institute has directly reimbursed employers, who continue to pay reservists their normal salaries. The Institute also compensates self-employed workers up to a specified maximum amount.[253] Besides this insurance system, Israeli legislation grants various tax breaks and other benefits to reservists, especially to those mobilized for lengthy periods. Nevertheless, the declining percentage of Israelis actually performing reserve duty has led some of those who do serve to complain about inferior pay, benefits, and other treatment.[254]

To minimize the economic disruption caused by mass reserve call-ups, Israel has established a series of mixed civilian-military committees to consider requests for deferment from reserve mobilization. Certain strategic industries and services have been declared so essential that their personnel regularly receive exemptions from reserve duty. Government pressure also has led Israeli universities to allow student reservists to postpone examinations and papers, receive special tutoring and photocopies of lecture notes, and repeat courses for free whenever their military commitments require them to miss an excessive number of classes.[255]

Despite these accommodations, the large-scale mobilization of reservists for protracted military operations has proven severely disruptive to Israel's economy and society. The diversion of much of the country's workforce causes serious labor shortages in certain sectors, a decline in economic activity due to a loss of markets and clients, and abrupt changes in the supply and demand for various products. Foreign investors and tourists also hesitate to enter an active war zone. These financial burdens are so great that, until recently, any widespread mobilization of reservists almost required Israel to go to war soon thereafter since the civilian economy would collapse under their prolonged absence. As the 1967 Six Day War illustrated, the social pressures ensuing from mass mobilization could also pressure the government into taking rapid military action.[256]

Israel's invasion of Lebanon in 1982 presented even more problems for the IDF manpower system, which posited only intermittent use of reservists in combat operations. Based on their experience in 1956, 1967, and 1973, Israeli military planners had anticipated that after a few days of victories, the United States and other foreign actors would pressure them to halt their advance and negotiate a ceasefire. For this reason, the IDF found it difficult to manage the burden of extended occupation duties following the offensive stage of the 1982 Lebanon intervention. Becoming entangled in Lebanon impaired the IDF's ability to prepare for future wars, and the reserve forces had a plethora of burdensome responsibilities. Among other missions, they assisted regular soldiers in countering the Syrian military, maintained order in occupied southern Lebanon, patrolled roads subject to guerrilla attacks, and prevented terrorist incursions into Israeli territory. The prolonged mobilization of reservists placed the overstretched IDF in a vulnerable strategic position.[257] These pressures led Israel to withdraw its military forces from Lebanon in May 2000.

As a result of its negative experience in Lebanon, the IDF tried to reduce the frequency of lengthy reserve deployments. Whereas in 1989 reservists served an average of 27 days in combat operations and 20 days in noncombat duties (i.e., maintenance and guard positions), the corresponding figures in 1994 were 21 and 13 days. During the 1983-97 period, the number of conscripted soldiers increased by 46.3 percent as the IDF sought to become less dependent on reservists by using more regular soldiers.[258] By the early 1990s, the number of summons to reserve duty had decreased considerably. In 1988, reservists spent a total of 9.8 million days on duty; by 1995, this number had decreased to less than 6 million.[259] The IDF also lowered the maximum age of reservists in combat units from 54 to 42 to ensure that only physically fit personnel served on active duty. The dramatically increased costs and time required to train soldiers to handle the latest advanced military technologies also led the IDF to rely more heavily on long-term professionals rather than reservists.[260] Those reservists who remained received more sophisticated and specialized training. Perhaps for these reasons, analysts estimated that in the late 1990s, roughly 10 percent of all reservists performed 80-90 percent of all active duty tasks designated for the reserve components.[261]

The Palestinian uprisings in the occupied territories—the first *Intifada* lasted from 1987 to 1993; the second *al-Aqsa Intifada* began in September 2000 and continues today—ended a decade-long decline in reserve call-ups. Although Israeli commanders preferred to use specially trained career professionals for delicate occupation tasks such as joint patrolling with units of the newly created Palestinian Authority (PA), the IDF's regular personnel proved insufficient both to police the territories and defend the country against possible threats from Syria, Lebanon, and Iran. When Palestinian terrorists began to launch widespread suicide attacks against Israeli civilians during the second *Intifada*, the government found it necessary to curtail most reserve training unrelated to counterterrorist and occupation missions. It also abandoned plans to shorten reserve duty.[262] By 2001, reservists comprised approximately one-third of the Israeli troops in the West Bank and roughly 15 percent of the troops in the Gaza Strip.[263]

The resulting increased mobilization of reservists for occupation duties generated unprecedented manifestations of dissatisfaction within their ranks. In early 2002, approximately 100 reservists organized a group protest against serving in the West Bank and Gaza Strip. They complained about an uneven distribution of unwelcome police duties among reserve units and about the perceived injustices associated with the occupation.[264] The authorities did not hesitate to punish reservists on duty who committed acts of disobedience. They argued that as citizens, reservists enjoy the opportunity to help determine their government through periodic democratic elections and therefore must obey its decisions. Notwithstanding these protests, in mid-2002 the IDF successfully mobilized 20,000-30,000 reservists in Operation HOMAT MAGEN ("Defense Wall"). These troops reentered PA-controlled territory in an effort to uproot the terrorist infrastructure that had been supporting a destructive wave of suicide bombings within Israel. Although the government refused to authorize major funding increases to improve reservists' training or equipment, it did create the new position of chief reserves officer, with the rank of brigadier, to ensure that a senior IDF commander would make reserve issues his or her sole responsibility. Previously, the deputy chief of staff managed reserve affairs as one of many duties.

The burden placed on reservists in the second *Intifada* led the government to form a special commission to examine the status of Israel's reserve components. In October 2005, this commission recommended drastically cutting the number of reservists assigned to police functions such as operating checkpoints, patrolling border infiltration points, and guarding Jewish settlements in the occupied territories. During that year, when most of the regular army became preoccupied with Israel's disengagement from the Gaza Strip, some 95 percent of enlisted reservists participated in security activities in the occupied territories. The October 2005 plan aimed to reduce the proportion of mobilized reservists engaged in occupation missions to 10 percent, while devoting more reservist training to preparing for conventional wars and other major emergencies. The expectation was that private security companies would assume the role of guarding Jewish settlements in the West Bank.[265] In accordance with this plan, the IDF dissolved some reserve units and activated a declining number of others for combat or guard duty during the first half of 2006. It also reduced the number of obligatory annual service days from 30 to 14 and lowered the maximum age for enlisted male reservists to 40. In 2005, Israel activated 30 percent of its reserve force. In 2006, it had planned to activate only 20 percent—one of the lowest percentages in Israeli history.[266]

The Second Lebanon War (July 12-August 14, 2006) required the Israeli government to mobilize thousands of reservists for urgent combat duty before the planned changes had come into effect. In fact, Hezbollah precipitated the war by kidnapping two reserve soldiers, Eldad Regev and Ehud Goldwasser, in a cross-border raid aimed at compelling a hostage exchange. Although the Israeli government did not order a large-scale mobilization of reservists until almost 2 weeks after the fighting began, the IDF eventually called up over 30,000 reservists, who played an increasingly important role in the ground war.[267] By the time the ceasefire took effect, reservists had suffered almost half of Israel's 117 military fatalities.[268]

The military's failure to inflict a decisive blow against Hezbollah led many reservists to protest about equipment shortages, inadequate pre-deployment training, poor military and political leadership, and other problems.[269] Some analysts believe the IDF and its reserve components had become excessively preoccupied with policing the occupied territories. In this view, because their training and operations focused so heavily on small-unit counterterrorist missions, the reservists had neglected to prepare adequately for large-scale conventional conflicts such as the war in Lebanon during the summer of 2006.[270] Another common criticism was that Israeli planners had placed excessive faith in air power and underestimated the need for the large ground forces supplied primarily by the IDF's reserve components.[271] Other observers vigorously disputed these assessments, either attributing the military's difficulties to different factors or arguing that the IDF performed better than its critics claim.[272]

Members of the Israeli government have acknowledged the legitimacy of some of these criticisms. For example, IDF Chief of Staff Lieutenant General Dan Halutz said in retrospect that he would have called up and trained reservists earlier in the conflict.[273] Other Israeli commanders explain that budgetary cuts and the expense of responding to the *Intifadas* had required them to reduce spending on reserve training, equipment, and logistical support.[274] Internal IDF committees, whose members include reservists, have already begun investigating the most important aspects of the country's performance in the Second Lebanon War, including the degree of preparedness in both the reserve and regular forces.

CHAPTER 11

THE RUSSIAN FEDERATION

In assessing Russia's current military reserve policies, a comparison with Soviet-era military manpower policies (*komplektovaniye vooruzhennikh sil'*) is instructive. Soviet doctrine and operational practices continue to influence the policies of the Russian Federation, whose senior officers were overwhelmingly educated and trained in Soviet military institutions. As one Russian defense analyst lamented, these continuities mean that the main difference between the current Russian military and its Soviet predecessor has been the "inferior quality" of the former.[275]

In many respects, the Soviet military's reserve components served as the linchpin around which the entire national military manpower system revolved. Soviet leaders placed a high priority on maintaining a large pool of well-trained military reservists. In their eyes, the Union of Soviet Socialist Republics' (USSR) victory in World War II resulted from its ability to mobilize more reservists than its opponents. Employing fewer reservists and more long-term professionals or short-term conscripts appeared impractical given the protracted, large-scale conflict anticipated by Soviet military planners. Sustaining a larger cadre of long-term professionals appeared too burdensome. In addition, although many conscripts learned useful technical skills (e.g., engineering, construction, machine maintenance) in the military that they could later use in corresponding civilian sectors, the USSR's labor-intensive economy could not afford the diversion of manpower that would have resulted from sustaining an even larger conscript force. Following centuries of Czarist tradition, the Soviet Union developed one of the largest conscription systems in history.[276] With few exceptions, millions of youth annually served in the Soviet armed forces. More importantly, they automatically joined the reserves upon completing their obligatory basic service.

The reserve mobilization model led Soviet analysts to adopt a different approach to military readiness than the United States. For the Soviet General Staff, high readiness meant being able to mobilize large numbers of reservists rapidly rather than having all active-duty units fully manned and equipped.[277] In American terms, the Soviets deliberately constructed a "hollow" army. Many units listed in the Soviet order of battle were intentionally undermanned. Some consisted of only a small administrative cadre with limited organic equipment. Soviet strategists developed detailed plans to enlarge these units with complements of mobilized reservists in a crisis. This system proved capable of mobilizing thousands of reservists during the Soviet military interventions in Czechoslovakia in 1968 and in Afghanistan in 1979.

Ensuring that reservists were adequately trained (as well as politically indoctrinated and subordinate to civilian control) became a priority of Soviet leaders. The over one million servicemen discharged annually from active duty guaranteed that millions of reservists would have up-to-date knowledge of Soviet tactics and equipment. Soviet law placed reservists into various categories depending on age, and required them to inform the authorities of changes in their residency and places of employment. The Soviet General Staff would then periodically recall them for refresher training, generally with decreasing frequency as they approached the maximum liability age (normally 50 years) for reserve duty.[278] (The Russian Federation continues to use this age-scaled system for reserve call-ups.) The obligatory use of internal passports; the extensive system of military commissariats responsible for administering the human, transportation, and other military assets in their jurisdictions; and the coercive powers of the Soviet police state ensured almost total compliance with these military notification, training, and mobilization requirements. The USSR also maintained an enormous professional military education system in order to train the active-duty and reserve officers required to lead the massive reserve manpower that would be mobilized in a crisis.

Following the USSR's collapse and the Cold War's end, many influential Russian officers and conservative defense analysts initially strived to sustain the potential to raise a large army (referred to as the "mobilization resource" or "mobilization reserve") capable of waging a protracted conventional conflict with NATO.[279] It soon became apparent, however, that Russia could not simply continue Soviet-era polices. Russia's disastrous experience during the first Chechen War of 1994-96—when the Army, despite supposedly having some 70 divisions in its order of battle, could initially only assemble a few ineffective "composite" units consisting of men who had never trained or served together—highlighted the acute need to establish a new personnel mobilization system more appropriate for modern Russian conditions.[280] The demise of the totalitarian system has decisively weakened the state's ability to force potential conscripts to serve. In addition, the Russian Federation's smaller population base and more severe demographic problems, as compared to the USSR, limit the number of potential conscripts.

Finally, Russians have proved unwilling to devote the tremendous financial and other resources that the Soviet Union bestowed on the Red Army.

The Russian government has struggled with the challenge of transitioning to a smaller, more professional military since the first Chechen War. Influenced by innovative reform proposals emanating from both younger officers and civilian defense analysts, Russian political and military leaders have repeatedly pledged to eliminate compulsory military service and transform the armed forces into an all- (or almost all-) volunteer force.[281] Yet, the Russian Ministry of Defense (MOD) still relies primarily on conscripts. Rather than restructure the military through extensive rebalancing or reorganization, which could initially require large government expenditures, the MOD has merely reduced its size, sometimes by eliminating units that existed largely on paper in any case. Today, Russia's armed forces still largely resemble a scaled-down version of the Red Army. The size of the active-duty military has declined from some five million during the Soviet period to slightly over one million, but volunteers account for only approximately one-seventh of the remaining personnel.[282]

In July 2006, President Putin signed a new law requiring that, starting in 2007, all Russian male draftees serve 18 months in the armed forces (down from the prior requirement of 24 months), except for certain occupations in the Navy, which require a longer term of service. The long-awaited Law on Alternative Service which the Duma passed in mid-2002, came into force in January 2004. It formally allows genuine conscientious objectors the right to undertake other forms of public employment instead of military service. In practice, however, the law's stiff provisions discourage draftees from using it. The legislation requires several years of low-paid public service and participants have little say in their place or type of employment. The authorities also reject many applications. Today, less than one thousand Russians undertake formal alternative service.[283]

The government has pledged to reduce the term of service for new conscripts to 1 year starting in January 2008, with 6 months of training at a military base and 6 months of service in an operational military unit. Defense Minister Sergey Ivanov has warned, however, that cutting in half the service commitment without increasing the number of volunteers could require drafting approximately twice as many conscripts — perhaps half a million per year.[284] Many analysts doubt that Russia can achieve this figure given its already staggering recruitment problems. Experts also expect the pool of available manpower to decrease drastically as a result of Russia's 20-year demographic crisis. The country has experienced plunging birth and soaring death rates, a sharp deterioration in living conditions and medical care, and a surge in chronic health problems among draft-eligible youth. Russia's Muslim minorities continue to have large families, but the growing percentage of Muslim recruits represents a mixed blessing due to their lower educational levels and potential susceptibility to radical Islamic doctrines.[285]

The unpopular war in Chechnya and frequent media reports of hazing and other abuses within the military have amplified Russia's recruitment problems. [286] Today, only about 1 in 10 eligible men actually receive induction into the Russian armed forces. For example, the spring 2004 draft yielded only 9.5 percent of those potentially available for military service.[287] An extraordinarily large number of potential draftees either receive legal exemptions (for reasons of health, education, etc.) or dodge the draft by feigning illness; buying phony educational deferments; going underground; or, most commonly, by bribing members of medical, university admission, or draft board commissions. The individuals unable to exploit these loopholes have tended to be less affluent, educated, and healthy than the average Russian male. They also have been more prone to drug use and other criminal behavior, making it difficult for their commanders to maintain discipline or conduct training.[288] As a result, less than one out of three inductees graduate from boot camp. Ivanov himself has expressed concern over the military reverting to a Bolshevik-era army of "workers and peasants" since everyone else manages to avoid serving.[289] Poor living conditions, frequent harassment of new recruits by second-year conscripts (known as *dedovschina*, or "rule of the granddads"), and other problems engender widespread dissatisfaction within the ranks and frequent desertions.[290] Whenever the MOD, hoping to improve the number and quality of servicemen, has moved to eliminate or reduce exemptions to conscription, sharp public and media reactions have forced its retreat. Surveys show that the Russian public overwhelmingly supports ending conscription and introducing other major reforms, even at the price of higher defense spending.[291]

Russian analysts have debated expanding the use of voluntary contract soldiers (*kontraktniki*) to reduce the need for conscripts. *Kontraktniki* are not precisely professional soldiers in the Western sense. Since 1992, these nonconscript soldiers and sergeants have served on multiyear contracts in return for much higher salaries than regular soldiers (who receive about

$3 a month), but many of them do not consider the military their long-term profession. For this reason, MOD officials often see them primarily as disposable short-term mercenaries rather than as a professional cadre that warrants costly training and education. The performance of many of the *kontraktniki* in Chechnya reinforced this perception. Motivated primarily by financial rewards rather than patriotism, they frequently deserted in dangerous situations or when, as happened frequently under Yeltsin, the government could not pay their salaries.[292]

The MOD might be able to attract more and better *kontraktniki* if it devoted more resources to recruitment (e.g., advertising) and offered volunteers higher salaries and benefits (especially better food and housing). The few hundred dollars a month *kontraktniki* now receive as salary, even combined with the in-kind value of their room and board, equates to less than what many of them could earn from safer civilian employment where they could also enjoy more flexible living conditions. In recent years, however, the MOD has sought to reduce the percentage of the defense budget devoted to meeting personnel and maintenance expenses, while increasing the share allocated to developing and procuring advanced conventional and strategic weapons.[293] This approach complicates recruiting, let alone efforts to transition completely to an all-volunteer force which MOD officials and Western analysts have concluded would cost hundreds of billions of dollars.[294] In addition, senior officers have resisted ending conscription since it would weaken their almost absolute control over conscripts, many of whom they treat like serfs. The Russian media is replete with stories of officers using the soldiers under their command for personal projects like refurbishing their dachas or hiring them out to other employers in return for money or favors.[295] A reduction in aggregate military personnel, moreover, would likely require involuntary retirements among Russia's traditionally top-heavy officer class.[296] Finally, ending conscription entirely would severely reduce the pool of readily available reservists, since far fewer Russians would have recent military experience.

The Putin administration's current transformation plan envisages creating a mixed system that in a few years would combine long-term professional soldiers, *kontraktniki* (who by 2008 will constitute a quarter of the total military establishment, and over half the Russian Army), and limited numbers of short-term conscripted servicemen.[297] Under this scheme, the total number of active-duty personnel would decline to approximately one million by 2016.[298] The planned force employment policy would exclude use of conscripts in conflict zones and anti-terrorism missions except during national emergencies. The MOD would instead deploy professional soldiers and *kontraktniki* to "hot spots" such as Chechnya and Central Asia (where Russia has several permanent military bases). These volunteers could also participate in UN- and NATO-led peacekeeping missions, such as those in the Balkans or Sudan. (These operations are popular among *kontraktniki* because of the high wages typically paid.) In early February 2005, the 15th Detached Peacekeeping Motorized Rifle Brigade—manned solely by *kontraktniki* and regular officers with good foreign-language skills—became operational. This special unit's main purpose is to work with NATO and other foreign militaries on international peacekeeping, search-and-rescue, and counterterrorist operations.[299]

It remains uncertain whether such long-term transformation plans will survive the presidential transition in 2008, when Putin is scheduled to leave office. Past promises to shorten conscription tours and increase the use of contract soldiers have been promptly forgotten. Nevertheless, since less comprehensive measures have proven insufficient to overcome recruitment and retention problems, incentives for fundamental reform will persist. For example, few individuals have taken advantage of the provision in Russian law that allows citizens of other members of the Commonwealth of Independent States (CIS) to obtain Russian citizenship by serving in the Russian armed forces for 3 years on a contract basis.[300] Although the new July 2006 law on military service abolishes or limits the grounds for many deferments, its practical effects in the face of widespread official corruption and public indifference remain unclear. During the month of the law's enactment, the military call-up did yield the desired number of conscripts, but their poor quality (especially their medical problems and low average education levels) led the authorities to induct fewer than half of them.[301] Federal, regional, and local bodies have proven unable to inculcate sufficient patriotism among Russian youth to motivate enough of them to join the armed forces. Many Russian analysts expect demographic, financial, and other imperatives to necessitate further reform efforts even if the MOD's current transformation plans are fully implemented.[302]

The MOD continues to organize full-scale training call-ups of reservists (colloquially referred to as "partisans") in all regions. A major task of the "Vostok-2003" exercise was practicing the mobilization of the reserves.[303] In 2005, President Putin authorized a training call-up of reservists in units of the regular military, the Ministry of Interior, the civil defense corps, the border guard, the Federal Security Service (FSB), and other federal security agencies for up to 2 months. In September 2006, the MOD organized SOUTHERN SHIELD 2006, a major exercise involving units in the Volga-Urals Military District (consisting of the Perm Territory, Udmurtia, and the Orenburg, Penza, Samara and Sverdlovsk regions). Reservists provided 3,500 of the 9,000 troops involved in the exercise.

The existing military service law permits the government to mobilize reservists until they reach the age of 50. The total duration of periodic training cannot exceed one 2-month call-up every 3 years. The law also limits the aggregate mobilization of reservists for training call-ups to 12 months in total for their entire period of service. Local government bodies and the MOD split the costs and coordinate the timing of routine training sessions. The MOD alone organizes urgent call-ups in order to check a region's readiness to mobilize forces in emergency situations. Within the MOD, the General Staff and the Military Inspectorate determine the specific tasks to be exercised during call-ups.[304]

During these routine training call-ups, reservists are organized into one or more separate units. They receive 2-week training classes tailored to updating the specialties they learned during their past conscript service. They also typically participate in live-fire shooting exercises. District military commissioners continue to complain that approximately one-third of all reservists ignore their call-up notices. Although Russian law guarantees reservists their jobs and average monthly pay, mobilized reservists are not compensated for their loss of large "bonuses" and other nontaxable compensation. Some Russian employers also discourage valuable workers from serving. The fine for ignoring a summons notice is small, and

Russia's preoccupied police rarely make tracking down dodgers a priority.[305]

Mass draft evasion has negatively affected the training of reserve officers. As a result of a 1989 law, men who graduate from college and complete a reserve officer training course can receive a reserve officer's commission without serving at all in the active-duty forces. They only need to complete a reserve officer's training course.[306] In order to help students avoid conscription, and allegedly to collect fees and bribes, higher educational institutions offer more reserve officer training programs today than during the Soviet period. Ivanov told the newspaper, *Argumenti i Fakti*, that "If half of these were shut down, this would have no effect on the Defense Ministry apart from saving it money. The military departments produce more than 50,000 reserve officers [annually]. The maximum number of officers whom we call up for 2 years is around 10,000."[307] The proliferation of these reserve officer programs appears to have reduced the quality of the average graduate—a worrisome development given that the military plans to rely heavily on reserve officers in any major conflict. In recent years, the MOD has had trouble retaining junior officers. Almost half of the Russian officers graduating from the country's military academies retire within 2-3 years because of their inadequate salaries, low social status, and other factors.[308]

The military effectiveness of Russia's current reserve components remains unclear. Russia still benefits from the legacy of the USSR's mass mobilization system. According to The International Institute for Strategic Studies (IISS), Russia has 20 million potential reservists, of which some 2 million have served on active duty within the last 5 years.[309] Yet, the country's reserve components undoubtedly have suffered from the general problems affecting the active-duty forces and Russian society more broadly. Although Russia's protracted conflict in Chechnya has enabled many reservists to gain "real world" operational experience, it is unclear how broadly any lessons learned from this conflict would apply to other types of missions. Maintaining peace in Sudan, for example, requires a different set of skills than killing guerrillas in the northern Caucasus. (The recent experience of Western militaries, however, has shown that such transitions do not present insurmountable obstacles.) The harmful effects of the Chechnya conflict on the morale and mental health of its veterans is an issue that remains understudied.

CHAPTER 12

CONCLUSION –
THE GLOBAL RESERVE REVOLUTION:
IMPLICATIONS FOR THE U.S. MILITARY

Several global forces are driving the worldwide changes in military reserve policies. First, the end of the Cold War has reduced the need for mass armies to wage protracted military campaigns on a continental scale. Military planners today require forces tailored to combat terrorism, conduct peace operations, and participate in other missions that, if not entirely new, have become increasingly prominent since 1990. Second, the advent of "post-modern" military organizations — which are more open to females, manned by volunteers rather than conscripts, and less differentiated from their civilian societies — has required considerable adjustments in recruiting, retention, and other human resources practices.[310] Third, despite the demands of the global war on terrorism, inflation-adjusted defense budgets remain well below Cold War levels in most countries. These funding limitations have led national military establishments to reduce their overall force structure substantially and, due to the belief that part-time soldiers cost less than regular troops, rely more heavily on their reserve components.

This increased reliance on reserve components presents national defense planners with many challenges. Recruiting and retaining reservists has become more difficult as many individuals have concluded they cannot meet the increased demands of reserve service. Reservists are increasingly deployed on foreign missions at a time when expectations regarding their contributions to the management of terrorist attacks, natural disasters, and other national emergencies are growing. Defense planners must also continue to refine the optimal distribution of skills and assets between regular and reserve forces. Finally, national governments must find the resources to sustain the increased use of reservists without bankrupting their defense budgets or undermining essential employer support for the overall concept of part-time soldiers with full-time civilian jobs.

Governments have adopted innovative responses to the complications associated with their growing use of reservists. To ease the pressures resulting from the increased convergence of reserve and active-duty deployment schedules, defense policymakers have tried to make rotation cycles more predictable and conducive to reservist lifestyles. For example, the British Ministry of Defence has formally adopted a policy of "intelligent selection" whereby it generally solicits volunteers for any operation before resorting to compulsory mobilization of reservists. Yet, MOD officials also cite a need to provide reservists with meaningful opportunities for participation in suitable military operations. They have sought to make reserve service more flexible and, by expanding the range of categories of reserve service, allow individuals greater opportunities to define their level of commitment. Other countries are also seeking to offer individuals a wider range of reserve service options and to facilitate their transfer among the various reserve and active duty components. Defense establishments are struggling to find a happy medium that will enable them to avoid overusing their reserve components while still keeping them "simmering."

The major military powers have widely adopted "total force" policies that treat their active and reserve components as integrated if not totally interchangeable elements—sometimes explicitly, sometimes just in practice, but always with major implications for a wide range of defense policies. National militaries are altering the relationship between their reserve and active-duty forces as they restructure both. Government policies increasingly treat mobilized reservists and regular forces similarly as they link more tightly the two components. They are harmonizing the reserve and active components' organizational structures, compensation packages, and rules and regulations. This convergence is especially evident in the ground forces, as seen in Australia, with its Hardened and Network Army (HNA) Plan, and in the United Kingdom, with its Future Army Structure initiative. Reservists now train and fight alongside their full-time colleagues on a daily basis, both at home and on foreign deployments. This integration will likely deepen as defense ministries take steps to facilitate transfers between their active-duty and reserve components, whether on a short-term basis or permanently. Nevertheless, many reservists still complain about their perceived second-class status regarding training opportunities, the quantity and quality of their equipment, and their treatment by field commanders when deployed on active duty.

The convergence in the roles and missions of countries' reserve and active components invariably raises questions over the appropriate distribution of skills between the two. Since part-time soldiers normally find it difficult to match the competencies of full-time professionals, governments have had to decide where the comparative advantages of reservists lie. Although reservists continue to perform traditional defense support functions, such as rear-area security and logistics, they have also assumed new responsibilities. These novel tasks often reflect the special skills and assets reservists can bring from their civilian lives to their military roles. In many high-technology fields, the capabilities available in a country's civilian economy exceed those readily available in the defense sector. For example, Chinese leaders have capitalized on their country's technology boom by organizing civilian information technology (IT) experts into special reserve information warfare units. Governments are developing databases to draw more effectively on the diverse range of reservists' skills that might contribute to military operations (e.g., IT experts for post-conflict infrastructure reconstruction missions). One problem with this approach is that many people join the reserves to pursue an occupation different from that of their civilian jobs. For this reason, several governments have adopted a formal policy of not requiring reservists to perform the same functions when on military duty as they do during their civilian jobs, except in an emergency.

Many countries have decided to keep certain skills predominantly in their reserve components, especially those they find impractical to maintain in sufficient quantity in their regular forces. For example, some medical specialties are rarely needed in peacetime, but become essential in wartime for helping severely wounded soldiers. In several cases, defense planners have assigned certain skills and missions exclusively to reservists. Although this practice helps keep costs down, the result has been a de facto globalization of the Abrams Doctrine: It has become nearly impossible for a country to go to war without mobilizing at least some of its reserve components.

Reservists are often seen as providing an essential link between a country's military profession and its civilian society. According to this view, reservists help transmit values between the two communities and limit undesirable divergences between them (though few people expect the military to try to seize power through coups in the nations under study). One result of this link is that national militaries have become more susceptible to broader societal trends. In most contemporary developed countries, for example, force planners must deal with declining birth rates, a growing population too old for military service, and a decreasing interest in military careers among young adults. Widespread changes in attitudes regarding women, however, have provided military recruiters with a new source of potential enlistees.

The declining size of many national reserve components, combined with an increased tendency for both regular and reserve forces to be drawn predominantly from certain—often disadvantaged—social groups, appears to have weakened the effectiveness of this military-civilian link. In response, foreign governments have restructured their reserve components to expand opportunities for military service. When the French government abolished compulsory military service, it even created a new reserve component, *la réserve citoyenne*, to sustain the link between the French nation and its armed forces that conscription was thought to have provided.

Another noteworthy development in civil-military relations has been reservists' increasingly important role in helping ensure their fellow citizens' safety and security during domestic emergencies. Governments are enhancing the capabilities, authorities, and missions of reservists to support civilian first responders following natural disasters, major accidents, and terrorist incidents. For example, Great Britain has created 14 new Civil Contingency Reaction Forces for use in such emergencies. Officials increasingly recognize that reserve components can supply unique niche capabilities in this area. Reservists can offer emergency responders advanced military capabilities and skills without requiring them to depend on overstretched regular forces, whose use at home could present legal and other problems. In addition, they often have excellent situational awareness due to their close ties to the surrounding civilian communities. As in the United States, however, foreign governments are still defining the proper roles of their militaries in the area of homeland security. The flawed response to Hurricane Katrina stimulated the American debate over the appropriate relationship between the Departments of Defense and Homeland Security. In France, China, and Russia, the authorities are also constantly reassessing the optimal division of responsibilities between their armed services and their paramilitary forces (especially the *gendarmerie*, the People's Militia, and the various Russian "power agencies") in managing domestic emergencies.

To ensure the ready availability of reserve units for homeland security and other priority missions, many countries—including Australia, China, Germany, Japan, and the United Kingdom—have developed "high-readiness" reserve components. Leaner militaries need to draw on reserves more rapidly than in the past, especially those units that supply HD/LD assets such as advanced IT support and nuclear, biological, and chemical capacities valuable for managing the consequences of WMD attacks. In return for higher financial compensation, these reservists agree to maintain exceptionally high readiness levels, typically by training more than average, and to commit to longer terms of service. Former active-duty service members are particularly valuable in this role given their familiarity with their country's most recent military doctrine and tactics. Even countries that have thus far resisted using a system of "tiered" or "graduated" readiness for their active-duty forces have been willing to apply this concept to their reserve units.

Providing these new capabilities invariably raises the financial costs of the reserve components at a time when most major military powers are cutting their defense budgets. National military establishments are reducing the size of both their active-duty and reserve components, but the cuts in the regular forces have typically been greater because reservists are thought to be more cost-effective. As governments spend more on training, equipping, and compensating reservists, however, the cost differential between the active and the reserve components decreases. A particularly expensive development has been the extension to reservists of health, education, and other benefits traditionally offered exclusively to regular soldiers. With the roles of reserve and regular forces increasingly indistinguishable on the battlefield, it becomes ever harder, both morally and politically, to deny reservists perquisites enjoyed by active duty soldiers. Overcoming recruitment and retention problems among reservists has also become expensive. To fill the ranks, governments have had to employ more recruiters, fund additional advertising, and provide more generous salaries and other benefits.

Governments also confront the increasingly expensive burden of sustaining employers' support for the expanding obligations on their reserve employees. On the one hand, the growing time commitment demanded from reservists for training and deployments has made them anxious about potential damage to their civilian careers, especially in terms of job promotion and retention. At the same time, competitive pressures have led even strongly patriotic employers to complain about the costs of supporting their frequently absent reservist employees. Most governments have responded to these pressures by both strengthening (or in some cases introducing for the first time) legal employment protections for reservists and providing much greater monetary compensation and other benefits to their employers. A recent development in some countries has been the formation of institutions like the United Kingdom's Supporting Britain's Reservists and Employers (SaBRE) program or France's *Conseil Supérieur de la Réserve Militaire*. Both organizations regularly solicit employers' views about the country's reserve policies and seek a solution that benefits employers, reservists, and governments alike.

Still another factor that complicates determining the relative cost-effectiveness of reservists is the difficulty of evaluating the tradeoff between the lower average salary of nonmobilized reservists and the various legal and practical restrictions on their use for certain operations (e.g., the typically longer time needed for their pre-deployment training). It is more cost-effective to keep certain infrequently needed specialist skills predominately in the reserve components, but recent experience has shown that defense departments often underestimate their requirements for these skills. Even when adequate aggregate capacity exists, miscalculations have resulted in the frequent mobilization of certain skilled reservists, leading to increasing recruitment and retention problems until governments "rebalance" their allocation of skills between the reserve and active components.

Finally, calculating the costs and benefits for the civilian economy is even more complex. When reservists perform their military duty, employers lose their immediate services and incur costs related to hiring replacement workers as well as paying for overtime and temporary coverage. Yet, some personnel expenses decline when the reservists go on leave. In addition, civilian employers often benefit from the tangible (e.g., special training) and intangible (e.g., leadership) skills that reservists acquire from their government-paid training. The net effect of these disparate factors varies depending on each case. Estimating their aggregate effect across the entire national economy is more complex — by an order of magnitude.

These trends have complicated efforts to assess the actual costs of countries' reserve components, especially since many expenses apply to their national armed forces as a whole. Fundamentally, it has become much more difficult to conduct cost-benefit analyses to determine the optimal active-reserve mix. In addition, limited understanding regarding the economic and other costs of maintaining and using reservists complicates assessing the advantages and disadvantages of possible changes in national reserve policies. For example, it is unclear whether extending additional financial benefits to reservists would improve national military capacity more than allocating those funds to regular active duty units. At present, policymakers and analysts tend to focus on the input side of the equation (e.g., how much is spent on each component) rather than on the outputs (how spending changes affect net military capacity) since evaluating the effectiveness of the latter is much harder.

The ongoing transformation in foreign countries' reserve forces creates both challenges and opportunities for U.S. defense planners. Since the end of the Cold War, the United States has found itself joining with a much broader range of coalition members in multinational military operations. The *National Security Strategy* and other core U.S. security documents stress the need to strengthen ties with friendly governments — both to help other countries defend themselves better (including against homeland security threats) and to contribute to the management of common challenges.[311] For example, the 2004 *National Military Strategy* argues that, to counter the global threat of terrorism, the United States must pursue "actions to shape the security environment in ways that enhance and expand multinational partnerships. Strong alliances and coalitions contribute to mutual security, tend to deter aggression, and help set conditions for success in combat if deterrence fails."[312] For this reason, the 2005 *National Defense Strategy* states that the DoD is "working to transform our international partnerships, including the capabilities that we and our partners can use collectively." The objective is "to increase our partners' capabilities and their ability to operate together with U.S. forces."[313] At a minimum, American defense planners will want to keep abreast of how key foreign militaries are changing their reserve components. In some cases, the DoD might consider applying suitable foreign innovations to its own reserve policies.

To improve the effectiveness of these multinational operations, American forces should take steps to enhance their interoperability with a wider range of potential partners. Most foreign governments recognize the value of undertaking multilateral military operations with the United States and should be open to cooperative initiatives embracing their reserve components. If better interoperability were the only concern, the United States and other countries could restructure their militaries to achieve symmetry in form, function, and organization. Realistically, however, the influence of history, geopolitics, threat perceptions, and other more weighty factors means that the basic structures of national militaries are largely fixed in the near future. For this reason, cooperative initiatives should aim for limited improvements that nevertheless could contribute meaningfully to actual military operations.

Reservists can help strengthen technical interoperability, which improves when engineers, weapons designers, and other defense experts work together to research and develop military technologies. More subjective forms of interoperability — such as an appreciation of the other parties' preferred tactics, techniques, and procedures — typically require close, frequent, and sustained military-to-military contacts. Since other demands on reservists' time invariably limit their ability to participate in long-term residential exchange programs such as the Army's Military Personnel Exchange Program, organizing additional opportunities for multinational military exercises, reciprocal visits, and other short-term contacts might prove more practicable. In special cases, resources might become available to fund longer-term exchanges for a few select reserve officers and other personnel. As with other issues, managing the competing time pressures on part-time soldiers requires compromises.

The United States and its traditional allies — NATO in Europe; Australia and Japan in Asia; and Canada closer to home — have made some progress in enhancing military interoperability through joint research and development programs, combined training and education, and other multilateral security cooperation initiatives. These existing activities now need to encompass countries' reserve components more comprehensively. National defense planners are increasingly assigning important military skills predominantly—and sometimes exclusively—to their reserve components. Even for short operations, commanders of multinational forces will likely need to access at least some of these skills, especially those relating to logistical support, information technology, communications and foreign languages. To sustain enduring peace and post-conflict reconstruction operations, governments will find it even more necessary to mobilize reservists to maintain sufficient manpower. Multinational operations would also benefit from the different perspectives and experiences reservists bring from their civilian careers and their stronger ties with local communities. Their background can prove especially useful in helping with the difficult transition from military- to civilian-led stability operations. By working with reservists, regular soldiers deepen their understanding of reserve issues and broader societal trends. Involving foreign reserve components more comprehensively in multilateral exercises with U.S. forces would facilitate mutual awareness of national military doctrines, concepts of operations, communications protocols, and other standards. Establishing additional mechanisms for dialogue on reserve issues would broaden opportunities for exchanging information regarding lessons learned, best practices, and future transformation plans.

The 2006 *QDR Report* notes that, "Recent operations have reinforced the need for U.S forces to have greater language skills and cultural awareness. It is advantageous for U.S. forces to speak the languages of the regions where the enemy will operate."[314] The DoD Defense Language Transformation Initiative, along with single Service initiatives to enhance cultural and language training among their personnel, aims to enable U.S. forces to work more effectively with foreign militaries.[315] For example, the U.S. Navy and Marine Corps are strengthening their foreign language training, cultural learning, and Foreign Area Officer program to "form a professional cadre of officers with regional expertise and language skills to provide support to Fleet Commanders, Combatant Commanders, and Joint staffs." The Navy sees these skills as essential for enabling its personnel to understand the "human terrain" of its international operating environment.[316] The new U.S. Chief of Naval Operations, Admiral Michael Mullen, has stressed that partnerships with foreign navies effectively give the United States access to a "1,000-ship navy." He told an audience in June 2006: "Imagine the power of having a cadre of foreign area officers who understand the language, build friendships, engender co-operation and undermine the very conditions often exploited by those who wish to fracture the peace."[317] Ties among American and foreign reservists could help develop international military relations in many areas, especially in those fields where they predominate—logistics, combat support, and intelligence. For example, U.S. reservists responsible for military intelligence (which includes linguists) could take advantage of their foreign counterparts' geographic expertise to generate insights concerning regional security developments, including data on local terrorist threats.

Many U.S. military exchange programs remain focused on traditional allies and have neglected new and potential partners. The United States needs to deepen defense contacts with foreign militaries that have not historically worked closely with American military forces. Although joint operations with the

Chinese PLA are unlikely to happen soon, joint U.S.-Russian operations are more plausible. Both Russia and the United States are contemplating humanitarian relief missions in distant and perhaps nonpermissive environments and even combined operations to secure or destroy WMD assets under risk of terrorist seizure. The International Military Education and Training Program (IMET) already provides training in English for Russian military officers and civilian MOD officials in peacekeeping operations, noncommissioned officer development, civil-military relations, and other topics designed to enhance such interoperability. These programs could be expanded and, with Beijing's approval, extended to the PLA.

The Russian and Chinese armed forces are admittedly difficult military partners. Their lack of transparency, distrust of American intentions, and other long-standing problems continue to complicate U.S. attempts at engagement.[318] The 2006 *QDR Report* rightly highlights the importance of "shaping the choices of countries at strategic crossroads" — a phrase used to describe Russia and China as well as India.[319] Despite these difficulties, efforts at cooperation should continue. Although it can take years to reshape former adversaries' deep-rooted perceptions and practices, delays will only postpone the achievement of this goal even further. The armed forces of China and Russia will remain important national actors for many years given their size, resources, and bureaucratic influence. It is precisely because Russia and China are neither allies nor adversaries of the United States that military-to-military contacts and other forms of bilateral defense diplomacy are both necessary and possible.[320]

Since 1993, many National Guard State Partnership Programs (SPP) have established collaborative defense relationships with former Soviet bloc countries. (The SPPs have since expanded to encompass countries which are new U.S. military partners in Asia and Latin America.) These programs now encompass a range of security cooperation activities including military exchanges, training opportunities, and joint programs to deal with such security threats as narcotrafficking and natural disasters. The activities are coordinated through the appropriate Theater Combatant Commander and U.S. embassy country teams. They aim to promote mutual understanding and trust, enhance participants' military capabilities, showcase American political and civilian values, and achieve other important objectives. The recent expansion of the military dialogue with China might allow for the establishment of an SSP with China, perhaps using the same informal mechanisms linking the New York National Guard to Russia.[321]

The protracted deployments of American military forces in the former Yugoslavia, Afghanistan, and Iraq have led the U.S. Government to develop new tools for such post-war occupation missions. In 2004, the Bush administration established the Office of the Coordinator for Reconstruction and Stabilization in the State Department. The Office aims both to strengthen U.S. civilian planning for stabilization operations and to improve interagency coordination during actual deployments. Its 55-member interagency staff has consisted of personnel on loan from DoD, the Central Intelligence Agency, and other U.S. Government offices as well as career State Department employees.[322] In November 2005, the DoD officially defined "Stability, Security, Transition, and Reconstruction (SSTR) Operations" as a "core U.S. mission" warranting equal priority with combat operations. The directive underscores the importance of promoting foreign language training, regional area expertise, and ties with foreign governments and nongovernmental organizations.[323]

Reservists appear particularly suited for foreign constabulary, peacekeeping, and post-conflict stability operations because these missions tend to require less advanced fighting skills and more civilian-type reconstruction, civil affairs, and related capabilities. To improve the foreign language proficiency and international awareness of U.S. military personnel, DoD will now require recipients of Reserve Officer Training Corps (ROTC) scholarships and Service Academy students to take courses in foreign languages. DoD also plans to create a 1,000-person Civilian Linguist Reserve Corps that would be readily available for military operations.[324] Its members would make excellent candidates for participation in foreign military exchanges. Since these reservists would already know their target language, moreover, they would not need to undertake lengthy language training in foreign countries — an impossibility for most reservists.

Through their security cooperation activities with foreign governments, reservists can also promote peacetime efforts to shape regional security environments. The focused Theater Security Cooperation Strategies of the regional combatant commands (e.g., U.S. Pacific Command) should take better advantage of their possible contributions. For the same reason, reservists could also assist with the U.S. Global Peace Operations Initiative designed to increase friendly governments' military capabilities and their interoperability with U.S. forces. Another way reservists can contribute to strengthening defense relationships between the United States and other countries is to establish liaison arrangements with foreign military headquarters and with foreign government agencies responsible for reserve affairs.

U.S. military exchange programs could also be better coordinated. The Office of the Secretary of Defense and the Joint Staff need to reduce redundancies, eliminate gaps, and exploit synergies in what remain largely individual Service-driven programs. Furthermore, DoD, the National Security Council, and other senior U.S. Government bodies could adopt additional measures to enhance coordination of international security interoperability efforts across the U.S. national security establishment.[325] DoD would also need to devote sufficient resources to entice greater participation in these efforts from both active and reserve members. For example, reservists who join in engagement activities with foreign militaries could receive such tangible benefits as credit for promotion and, where possible, subsequent assignments that utilize their experience and expertise. If American defense planners genuinely appreciate the need to expand contacts with foreign militaries, including their reserve components, they need to show it.

Besides optimizing the participation of reservists in exchanges and other mechanisms to promote military cooperation between the United States and potential coalition partners, DoD should also evaluate certain foreign reserve practices to ascertain if they might profitably be applied, suitably modified, to the U.S. reserve components. Any such application would need to take into account the differences in countries' military commitments, active/reserve force mix, human and financial resources, and other criteria—including the different implicit "social compact" underpinning the roles of each nation's citizen soldiers.

First, it might make sense to establish a formal category of "high-readiness" reserves who—in return for greater financial benefits, better training, and more opportunities to serve—would agree to undergo additional mandatory training and deploy immediately if needed. The 2006 *QDR Report* states that DoD will "[d]evelop select reserve units that train more intensively and require shorter notice for deployment."[326] The Military Services have already launched several pilot programs to expand the number and types of variable reserve participation at the unit level. More comprehensively, they have restructured reservists' deployment schedules, making only a selected group of them subject to mobilization during certain time periods. These units undergo concentrated training preparation in order to reduce the time required for mobilization and deployment. Unlike a traditional tiered-readiness system, however, the Service rotation systems for both the active and reserve components anticipate that over time all military personnel will endure periods of high readiness. The DoD should evaluate whether the increase in predictability and preparedness that could result from formally designating certain military personnel as "high-readiness" reservists would outweigh the corresponding monetary costs and the possible invidious effects on other reservists, who now would be seen, even if not formally so labeled, as "low readiness" components. Now that the United States is adjusting the length of its reserve deployments, moreover, perhaps DoD planners should consider the Israeli practice of more frequently rotating reserve units in and out of combat theaters. Such a practice helps ameliorate overuse of reservists, but may prove impractical given the global extent of U.S. military deployments. It is considerably easier for IDF reservists to return to combat zones in neighboring territories than for American reservists based in the United States to move back and forth to overseas operations.

Second, DoD might wish to evaluate in greater detail the applicability of certain foreign innovations to strengthen employer backing for reserve participation. The Uniformed Services Employment and Reemployment Rights Act (USERRA), adopted in 1994, has helped achieve its three objectives of facilitating part-time military service by full-time civilian employees, guaranteeing the reemployment of discharged military personnel, and preventing discrimination against individuals because of their military service—primarily by acting as an ombudsman to mediate disputes. Nevertheless, the United States might benefit from adopting certain foreign practices in this area. For example, the United States might want to organize a formal body like France's CSRM that would periodically arrange large-scale conferences of government officials, employers, and other interested parties to discuss the condition of the reserve components and recommend possible improvements. In addition, U.S. entities such as the National Committee for Employer Support of the Guard and Reserve (ESGR)—a DoD staff group that has established a nationwide network of voluntary local support committees—might consider adopting certain elements of Britain's SaBRE program to help sustain private sector support for reservists and facilitate resolution of employer-employee problems concerning employees' military obligations.[327] Finally, although DoD has abandoned plans to establish an insurance scheme designed to compensate reservists or employers who suffer losses from the mobilization of their reserve employees, Israel, Japan, and other countries have acquired several years of experience with such subsidy programs that might provide insights for any future U.S. Government endeavors in this area.

Third, the U.S. Government might also wish to follow Canada, France, and other countries in developing new initiatives to bolster high school recruitment into the reserve components. Since the late 1990s, France has required all French citizens between the ages of 16 and 18 to spend a day at a nearby public facility (often a military base) at the government's expense to learn about the French defense establishment, including opportunities to serve in the reserve components. Only those who complete the program receive the documents they need to take the national entrance examinations required for higher public education institutions and many government jobs. Although DoD reserve recruiters have a broad range of techniques at their disposal, they might benefit from adopting a more extensive program designed to expose young Americans to career opportunities in the military and its reserve components.[328]

More generally, foreign experience might help U.S. human resource managers as they attempt to apply the "continuum of service" concept to the U.S. military. This concept was advocated most prominently in the December 2002 "Review of Reserve Component Contributions to National Defense" study, mandated by the 2001 QDR. The concept seeks to deemphasize the inflexible binary choices commonly available in the past (active/reserve; full-time/part-time; etc.). Instead, it attempts to offer military personnel expanded opportunities to move into, between, and within active and especially reserve duty categories—with varying time commitments and other obligations in return for corresponding levels of benefits—as their personal interests and circumstances evolve.[329] On the other hand, attempting to copy France's innovative Citizen

Reserve would probably not prove useful given the lack of a conscription tradition in the United States. Furthermore, the United States already has a range of intermediary bodies (think tanks, military associations, etc.) that attempt to maintain a link between U.S. society and its armed forces. In any case, the U.S. National Guard already performs many of the representational and public education functions that the French have assigned to the *réserve citoyenne*.

Finally, the growing number and prominence of private contractors on the battlefield has complicated the management of American military operations. For example, the higher take-home pay received by many civilian specialists may have led some highly trained military personnel to join these private sector firms rather than the reserves.[330] Another problem associated with the use of civilian contractors is their lesser accountability as compared with mobilized reservists, who fall under the military chain of command and the Uniform Code of Military Justice (UCMJ). On several occasions in Iraq, private firms have postponed or abandoned their tasks when their operating environment became excessively dangerous.[331] The rules of engagement for contractors remain unclear, as do the law enforcement mechanisms that apply to them. DoD representatives currently depict private contractors and reservists as two of the four key elements of its Total Force (along with its Active Component and civilian employees).[332] In October 2005, the Department issued more detailed guidance for some of these questions—such as when military personnel are obliged to defend contractors, what type of armaments contractors can carry, and when private security contractors can guard U.S. or allied facilities or personnel.[333]

Thus far, the United States and other governments have relied on a combination of patriotism and

141

bonuses to discourage reservists from joining civilian contractors. The British, however, have established the innovative category of "Sponsored Reserves" to ensure that certain key civilian contractors deploy as reservists in support of foreign military missions. These individuals are liable for mobilization when their skills are required for military operations, such as when their technical expertise is needed to maintain complex weapons systems. U.S. defense planners, who depend more on private contractors than perhaps any other country, have just begun a pilot program to assess how a sponsored reserve scheme might work in the Air Force Reserve in such fields as intelligence, space operations, and U.S.-based logistics.[334] DoD analysts should comprehensively evaluate the British system, including its possible contribution to other missions. Ideally, sponsored reservists might help secure the presence of essential civilian support assets even in non-permissive environments such as Iraq. Their presence might also allow for the expanded use of private contractors in cases when the nation's inherently limited number of reservists is needed for more urgent duties—as has increasingly become the case.

ENDNOTES

1. Office of the Deputy Assistant Secretary of Defense for Reserve Affairs, *Rebalancing Forces: Easing the Stress on the Guard and Reserve*, Washington, DC: January 15, 2004; and Christine E. Wormuth *et al.*, *The Future of the National Guard and Reserves: The Beyond Goldwater-Nichols Phase III Report*, Washington, DC: Center for Strategic and International Studies, July 2006, p. 92.

2. U.S. Department of Defense, *Strategy for Homeland Defense and Civil Support*, Washington, DC: June 2005, p. 35.

3. For a discussion of these various legal issues in the homeland defense context, see Army National Guard, *National Guard Homeland Defense White Paper: September 11, 2001, Hurricane Katrina, and Beyond*, Washington: October 11, 2005, at *www.arng.army.mil/Publications/HLD%20White%20Paper_11OCT05_Final Version.pdf*; and Robert Λ. Preiss, "The National Guard and Homeland Defense," *Joint Force Quarterly*, No. 36, December 2004, pp. 72-78.

4. For more on this internal DoD debate, see Greg Jaffe, "Katrina Will Shape Military Debate," *Wall Street Journal*, September 12, 2005.

5. Phillip S. Meilinger, "Airpower and the Reserve Components," *Joint Force Quarterly*, No. 36, December 2004, p. 58.

6. CBRNE includes CBRN agents plus high explosives.

7. Michael O'Hanlon, "The Roles of DoD and First Responders," in Michael d'Arcy *et al.*, *Protecting the Homeland 2006/2007*, Washington, DC: Brookings, 2006, p. 118.

8. These problems are discussed in the Reserve Forces Policy Board, Office of the Secretary of Defense, *Mobilization Reform: A Compilation of Significant Issues, Lessons Learned and Studies Developed since September 11, 2001: A Summary of Significant Issues, Recommendations and Actions toward Mobilization Reform*, Washington, DC: October 2003; and U.S. Government Accountability Office, *DoD Actions Needed to Improve the Efficiency of Mobilizations for Reserve Forces*, Washington, DC: August 21, 2003. Specific problems with the compensation system for the U.S. reserve components are reviewed in Cindy Williams, *Transforming the Rewards for Military Service*, Cambridge, MA: Security Studies Program, Massachusetts Institute of Technology, September 2005,

pp. 26-27; and U.S. Government Accountability Office, *Military Pay: Army Reserve Soldiers Mobilized to Active Duty Experienced Significant Pay Problems*, Washington, DC: U.S. Government Accountability Office, August 2004. For a study that suggests that fewer reservists than believed may suffer a loss of earnings when mobilized, see David S. Loughran *et al.*, *Activation and the Earnings of Reservists*, Santa Monica, CA: RAND, 2006.

9. Some of the financial problems encountered by reservists who are self-employed or own small businesses (an estimated 6-7 percent of National Guard members) are reviewed in Amy Joyce, "Baghdad and Bust: Small-Business Owners Defending America are Losing Their Shirts," *Washington Post*, June 5, 2005.

10. U.S. Army Force Management School, *Reserve Components of the United States Military: An Executive Primer*, Fort Belvoir, VA: May 26, 2006, p. 8.

11. U.S. Department of Defense, *Quadrennial Defense Review Report*, Washington, DC: February 6, 2006, p. 76.

12. U.S. Army Reserve, "Six Imperatives of Army Reserve Transformation," at *www.armyreserve.army.mil/ARWEB/NEWS/20060915.htm*.

13. Lieutenant General James R. Helmly, *Army Reserve 2005 Posture Statement*, Washington, DC: March 2005, p. 7.

14. Lieutenant General James R. Helmly, *Army Reserve 2006 Posture Statement*, Washington, DC: March 2006, pp. 11-12, 15.

15. Jen DiMascio, "Schoomaker Articulates Philosophy for a 'Fully Resourced Army,'" *Inside the Army*, January 16, 2006.

16. Details on the ARFORGEN process appear in both the *Army Reserve 2005 Posture Statement*, pp. 8-9; and the *Army Reserve 2006 Posture Statement*, p. 11.

17. *Quadrennial Defense Review Report*, p. 43. Additional details on the new structure can be found in United States Army, *2006 Posture Statement*, Washington, DC: February 10, 2006, pp. 8-9.

18. Albert C. Zapanta, "Transforming Reserve Forces," *Joint Force Quarterly*, No. 36, December 2004, p. 71.

19. H. Steven Blum, "A Vision for the National Guard," *Joint Force Quarterly*, No. 36, December 2004, pp. 24-29. See also Albert C. Zapanta, "Regarding Reserve Component Transformation and Relieving Stress on the Reserve Component," testimony before the House Armed Services Committee, March 31, 2004.

20. "Reserve Components of the United States Military: An Executive Primer," pp. 27-28.

21. *Army Reserve 2006 Posture Statement*, pp. 7, 13.

22. Hans Binnendijk and Gina Cordero, "Transforming the Reserve Component," in Hans Binnendijk *et al.*, eds., *Transforming the Reserve Component: Four Essays*, Washington, DC: Center for Technology and National Security Policy, National Defense University, February 2005, pp. 3-4. In 2004, approximately 70 percent of the U.S. military police capability resided in the U.S. reserve components. Richard B. Meyers, "A Word From the Chairman," *Joint Force Quarterly*, No. 36, December 2004, p. 7.

23. The USAF reservists are especially useful for F-16, B-52, A-10 and tanker missions. See James Kitfield, "Guard and Reserve in a Time of War," *Air Force Magazine*, Vol. 87, No. 7, July 2004, pp. 22-28.

24. Gordon I. Peterson, "Seapower and the Reserve Components," *Joint Force Quarterly*, No. 36, December 2004, pp. 51-52.

25. These injunctions appear in a number of Rumsfeld-authored "Snowflake" memoranda to other senior DoD officials, cited in Reserve Forces Policy Board, *Mobilization Reform: A Compilation*, pp. 5-6.

26. *Quadrennial Defense Review Report*, p. 76.

27. U.S. Department of the Navy, "SECNAV Posture Statement: Providing the Right Force for the Nation Today ... While Preparing for the Uncertainties of Tomorrow," March 1 2006, at *www.navy. mil/navydata/people/secnav/winter/secnav_posture_statement.pdf*, p. 12; and U.S. Air Force, "The U.S. Air Force Posture Statement 2006," at *www.af.mil/library/posture/2006/forceintegration.html*, section on Total Force Integration.

28. *2006 Army Posture Statement*, p. 9.

29. *Quadrennial Defense Review Report*, p. 77.

30. Secretary of State for Defence, *Delivering Security in a Changing World: Future Capabilities*, London: Ministry of Defence, July 2004, p. 10.

31. "UK Defence: Reserves," *Defence Professionals in the UK and France*, at *www.dasasurveys.mod.uk/php/dp/index.php?c=2&s=6&1=e nglish&m=english*.

32. For information on the Regular Reserve, see "Types of Reservist and Manpower Strength," at *www.armedforces.co.uk/army/listings/l0070.html*.

33. The International Institute for Strategic Studies, *The Military Balance: 2007*, London: Routledge, 2007. See also Lord Drayson, Parliamentary Under-Secretary, Defence Procurement, Ministry of Defence, "Territorial Army: Rebalancing," House of Lords debates, March 23, 2006, at *www.theyworkforyou.com/lords/?id=2006-03-23b.386.0&m=100070*.

34. Sjouke de Jong, *NATO's Reserve Forces*, London: Brassey's, 1992, p. 92.

35. See also Peter Viggers, "Reserve Forces—The Nation's Insurance Policy: How the Conservatives Should Repair the Damage," *RUSI Journal*, Vol. 148, No. 1, February 2003, pp. 68-69.

36. Ministry of Defence, "Rebalancing Will Make TA More Relevant and Capable," *Defence News*, March 23, 2006, at *www.mod.uk/DefenceInternet/DefenceNews/DefencePolicyAndBusiness/RebalancingWillMakeTaMoreRelevantAndCapable.htm*. See also "Territorial Army in the Future Army Structure, FAS," at *www.armedforces.co.uk/army/listings/l0134.html*.

37. Information on the Royal Naval Reserve is available at *www.royal-navy.mod.uk/server/show/nav.2717*. Information on the RMR is available at *www.royal-navy.mod.uk/server/show/nav.2975*.

38. The Secretary of State for Defence, *Delivering Security in a Changing World: Supporting Essays*, London: His Majesty's Stationary Office, 2003, p. 8.

39. Royal Navy, "Frequently Asked Questions," April 26, 2004, at *www.royal-navy.mod.uk/server/show/conWebDoc.449/changeNav/3533*.

40. The Secretary of State for Defence, *Delivering Security in a Changing World*, p. 11.

41. Matthew Uttley, "Private Contractors on Deployed Military Operations: Inter-Agency Opportunities and Challenges," *Heritage Lecture* No. 972, October 31, 2006, p. 5.

42. Directorate of Reserve Forces and Cadets, *Future Use of the UK Reserve Forces*, February 7, 2005, at *www.sabre.mod.uk/files/pdf/Future_Reserve_Forces.pdf*.

43. "Thinning the Ranks," *The Economist*, July 24-30, 2004, p. 54.

44. "About Defence: British Reserve Forces," at *www.mod.uk/ DefenceInternet/AboutDefence/Organisation/KeyFactsAboutDefence/ BritainsReserveForces.htm.*

45. National Audit Office, *Ministry of Defence Reserve Forces,* London: The Stationary Office, March 28, 2006, pp. 8-9.

46. *Ministry of Defence Reserve Forces,* p. 8.

47. "About Defence: British Reserve Forces," at *www.mod.uk/ DefenceInternet/AboutDefence/Organisation/KeyFactsAboutDefence/ BritainsReserveForces.htm.*

48. The Secretary of State for Defence, *Delivering Security in a Changing World: Defence White Paper,* London: His Majesty's Stationary Office, 2003, p. 8.

49. Additional information on the homeland defense and security roles of the British reservists is provided in J. R. Thomson, "Mounting Offshore Operations Using the Reserve Forces and How it Impacted on Homeland Defence and Security — the United Kingdom Experience," *Journal of Military and Strategic Studies,* Vol. 7, No. 2, Winter 2004, at *www.jmss.org/2004/winter/articles/thomson. pdf.*

50. Christopher Dandeker. "Flexible Forces and the Regular/ Reserve Mix: the Case of the Territorial Army," in *Brassey's Defence Yearbook 1998,* The Centre for Defence Studies, ed., King's College, *Brassey's Defence Yearbook 1995,* London: Brassey's, 1995, p. 19.

51. "Types of Reservist and Manpower Strength," at *www. armedforces.co.uk/army/listings/l0070.html.*

52. The three main call-up powers provided by the Reserve Forces Act are described in NATO National Reserve Forces Committee, "National Reserve Forces Status: United Kingdom," at *www.nato.int/nrfc/database/uk.pdf.*

53. National Audit Office, *Ministry of Defence Reserve Forces,* London: The Stationary Office, March 28, 2006, p. 20.

54. *Ministry of Defence Reserve Forces,* pp. 3, 14-15, 18. For example, TA members of the Royal Signals are trained to operate a smaller number of communications systems than their Regular counterparts. In addition, the Royal Navy Reserve has no dedicated training ships, and has had difficulty gaining use of regular Royal Navy vessels for reserve training.

55. Ministry of Defence, "Employee Notification," at *www. en.mod.uk/output/page196.asp.*

56. Details regarding SaBRE are available at *www.sabre.mod. uk*.

57. The Secretary of State for Defence, *Delivering Security in a Changing World*, p. 10.

58. Directorate of Reserve Forces and Cadets, *Future Use of the UK's Reserve Forces,* London: February 7, 2005, p. 3.

59. National Audit Office, *Ministry of Defence Reserve Forces*, London: The Stationary Office, March 28, 2006, p. 36. "Simmering" is "a situation where the Territorial Army will continue to be used on operations at a certain level, even where the scale of operations may not strictly require reserves, to maintain a culture where Reservists can expect to be deployed and to sustain motivation," p. 65.

60. SaBRE, "Mobilisation: Telling Your Employer," at *www. sabre.mod.uk/output/Page55.asp*.

61. Michael Smith, "War Blamed as 6,000 Quit Territorial Army," *The Sunday Times*, October 30, 2005.

62. Charles Heyman, ed., *Jane's World Armies*, No. 15, London: Jane's Information Group, June 2004, pp. 915, 921.

63. Ian Bruce, "Concern over Falling TA Recruitment as More Part-Timers Deployed," *The Herald,* Glasgow, March 29, 2005.

64. As late as 1994, France's official defense White Paper, *Livre Blanc sur la Défense*, reaffirmed the importance of conscription: "National service . . . is still the recruitment method best suited to the scope and framework of the strategy, objectives and defense policy adopted by France, as well as the means used to accomplish them. This is reflected by the choice of a mixed system, combining professionals and conscripts," p. 94, at *lesrapports. ladocumentationfrancaise.fr/BRP/944048700/0001.pdf*.

65. Anthony H. Cordesman, *NATO's Central Regional Forces: Capabilities, Challenges, Concepts*, London: Jane's, 1988, p. 206.

66. David C. Isby and Charles Kamps, Jr., *Armies of NATO's Central Front*, London: Jane's, 1985, p. 162.

67. Information on the two components is available at Ministère de la Défense, "La réserve opérationnelle et la réserve citoyenne," at *www.defense.gouv.fr/sites/defense/base/dossiers/la_ reserve_operationnelle_et_la_reserve_citoyenne*.

68. "Reserve Opérationnelle: Conditions d'accés," September 29, 2005, at *www.reserves.terre.defense.gouv.fr/spip-unites/article-v2.php3?id_article=40.*

69. Ministère de la Défense, "La réserve en chiffres," 2007, *http://www.defense.gouv.fr/defense/layout/set/popup/content/view/full/23381.*

70. J. L. Betin, "2003 French Army OOB," November 3, 2003, at *www.warfarehq.com/articles/toaw_articles/2003FrenchOOB.shtml.*

71. French documents want to replace the "*reserve de masse*" with a "*reserve d'emploi.*"

72. Loi n° 99-894 du 22 octobre 1999 portant organisation de la réserve militaire et du service de la défense, article 19, at *www.defense.gouv.fr/sites/csrm/presentation/organigramme/les_textes/la_loi/loi_n99-894_du_22_octobre_1999/.*

73. Loi n° 2006-449 du 18 avril 2006 modifiant la loi n° 99-894 du 22 octobre 1999 portant organisation de la réserve militaire et du service de défense, 1, at *www.legifrance.gouv.fr/WAspad/UnText eDeJorf?numjo=DEFX0500010L.*

74. Assemblee Nationale, *Rapport relative a la programmation militaire pour les annees 2003 a 2008*, November 20, 2002, at *www.assemblee-nationale.fr/12/rapports/r0383.asp.*

75. Ministère de la Défense, "Etat sur la réserve opérationnelle, contrats ESR," at *www.defense.gouv.fr/sites/csrm/presentation/le_secretaire_general/composition_de_la_reserve_operationnelle.*

76. David A. Fulghum, "French Military Reserve Strength Increases," *Aviation Week & Space Technology*, Vol. 159, No. 18, November 3, 2003, p. 57.

77. M. Guy Teissier, "Rapport fait au nom de la commission de la défense nationale et des forces armées sur le projet de loi, n° 187 relatif à la programmation militaire, pour les années 2003 à 2008," November 25, 2002, p. 55, at *www.assemblee-nationale.com/12/pdf/rapports/r0383.pdf.*

78. Loi n° 2006-449 du 18 avril 2006 modifiant la loi n° 99-894 du 22 octobre 1999 portant organisation de la réserve militaire et du service de défense, 1, at *www.legifrance.gouv.fr/WAspad/UnText eDeJorf?numjo=DEFX0500010L.*

79. Ministère de la Défense, "La réserve en gendarmerie," *http://www.defense.gouv.fr/gendarmerie/enjeux_defense/lien_armees_nation/reserves/la_reserve_en_gendarmerie.*

80. Alan Ned Sabrosky, "France," in Douglas J. Murray and Paul R. Vioti, eds., *The Defense Policies of Nations: A Comparative Analysis*, second edition, Baltimore: Johns Hopkins University Press, 1989, p. 246.

81. "France," in *Defense & Foreign Affairs Handbook*, Washington, DC: International Strategic Studies Association, 2004, pp. 607-608.

82. Ministère de la Défense, "Les réserves de la gendarmerie," at *www.defense.gouv.fr/sites/gendarmerie/enjeux_defense/lien_armee_nation/reserves/les_reserves_de_la_gendarmerie*.

83. Ministère de la Défense, "Les Réserves de l'armée de Terre," October 6, 2005, at *www.reserves.terre.defense.gouv.fr/spip-unites/article-v2.php3?id_article=47*.

84. "Volunteers versus Conscripts: The Transformation of NATO Forces," *IISS Strategic Comments*, Vol. 4, No. 10, December 1998.

85. Mehmet Emre Furtun, "Military Trends in France: Strengths & Weaknesses," Washington, DC: Center for Strategic and International Studies, July 26, 2004, p. 2, at *64.233.161.104/search?q=cache:gehL-dTKsvIJ:www.csis.org/burke/trends_france.pdf+Military+Trends+in+France:+Strengths+ percent26+Weaknesses&hl= en&gl=us&ct=clnk&cd=1*.

86. See, for example, "La réserve militaire opérationnelle," at *www.defense.gouv.fr/sites/air/votre_espace/la_reserve_militaire/la_reserve_militaire_operationnelle*.

87. Ministère de la Défense, "La réserve opérationnelle et La réserve citoyenne," at *www.defense.gouv.fr/sites/defense/base/dossiers/la_reserve_operationnelle_et_la_reserve_citoyenne*.

88. Ministère de la Défense, *Rapport d'évaluation de l'état de la réserve militaire en 2004*, Paris: June 2005, p. 6, at *www.defense.gouv.fr/portal_repository/563073969__0001/fichier/getData*.

89. Loi relative à la programmation militaire 2003-2008, January 27, 2003, at *www.legifrance.gouv.fr/html/actualite/actualite_legislative/decrets_application/2003-73.htm*.

90. National Audit Office, *Ministry of Defence Reserve Forces*, London: The Stationary Office, March 28, 2006, p. 53.

91. Guillaume Parmentier, "France," in Yonah Alexander, ed., *Counterterrorism Strategies: Successes and Failures of Six Nations*, Washington, DC: 2006, pp. 54, 64-65.

92. Ministère de la Défense, "La réserve en chiffres," 2007, *http://www.defense.gouv.fr/defense/layout/set/popup/content/view/ full/23381.*

93. Charles Heyman, ed., *Jane's World Armies*, London: Jane's Information Group, June 2004, p. 300.

94. Loi n° 2003-73 du 27 janvier 2003 rélative a la programmation militaire pour les annes 2003 a 2008, at *www.legifrance.gouv.fr/ WAspad/UnTexteDeJorf?numjo=DEFX0200133L,* section 3.3.

95. Ministère de la Défense, *Les employeurs et la réserve*, Paris: Observatoire Social de la defense, June 2004, p. 71, at *www.defense. gouv.fr/portal_repository/596355627__0001/fichier/getData*, p. 6.

96. Ministère de la Défense, "Journée nationale du réserviste 2005," at *www.defense.gouv.fr/sites/rnd/levenement/journee_ nationale_du_reserviste/journee_nationale_du_reserviste_2005/.*

97. Embassy of France in the United States, "Reform of French National Defense," June 12, 2001, at *www.info-france-usa.org/ printfriendly/atoz/ref_def_pf.asp.*

98. Additional information on the CSRM is available at *www. defense.gouv.fr/sites/csrm/.*

99. *Ibid.*, p. 6.

100. Loi n° 2005-1720 du 30 decembre 2005 de finances rectificative pour 2005, at *www.defense.gouv.fr/portal_ repository/1791705986__0002/fichier/getData.*

101. Ministère de la Défense, *Les employeurs et la réserve*, p. 71.

102. Peter Struck, *The Bundeswehr Reservist Concept*, Berlin: Bundesministerium der Verteidigung, September 10, 2003.

103. For more on the conscription issue, see Martin Kanz, "Dismissing the Draft: Germany Debates its Military Future," *Harvard International Review*, Vol. 24, No. 4, Winter 2003, pp. 37-41; and Cindy Williams, "From Conscripts to Volunteers: NATO's Transitions to All-Volunteer Forces," *Naval War College Review*, Vol. 58, No. 1, Winter 2005, pp. 35-62.

104. The International Institute for Strategic Studies, *The Military Balance: 2007*, London: Routledge, 2007, p. 116.

105. Peter Struck, *Verteidigungspolitische Richtlinien für den Geschäftsbereich des Bundesministers der Verteidigung*, Berlin: Bundesministerium der Verteidigung, May 21, 2003, especially sections I and II.

106. Die Bundesregierung, "Die Bundeswehr 2010 nimmt Gestalt an," at *www.bundesregierung.de/en/artikel-,10001.913163/ Die-Bundeswehr-2010-nimmt-Gest.htm*. See also Tom Dyson, "German Military Reform 1998-2004: Leadership and the Triumph of Domestic Constraint over International Opportunity," *European Security*, Vol. 14, No. 3, September 2005, p. 380.

107. "Neue Aufgabe, neue Strukturen," *www.bundeswehr.de/ forces/reserve/041129_transformation.php*.

108. Federal Ministry of Defense, "Conceptual and Structural Parameters," February 28, 2005, at *www.bmvg. de/portal/a/bmvg/kcxml/04_Sj9SPykssy0xPLMnMz0vM0Y_ QjzKLt4w39XEFSUGYjvqRaGJGpuYIsaDUPH1vfV-P_NxU_ QD9gtzQiHJHR0UAj – PAw!!/delta/base64xml/L2dJQSEvUUt3Q S80SVVFLzZfOV8zVkI!?yw_contentURL=/C1256F1200608B1B/ W268SHT2252INFOEN/content.jsp*.

109. Jean R. Tartte, "National Security," in Eric Solsten, ed., *Germany: A Country Study*, Washington, DC: Library of Congress, 2005, chapter 9.

110. NATO National Reserve Forces Committee "National Reserve Forces Status: Germany," at *www.nato.int/nrfc/database/ germany.pdf*.

111. Bundeswehr, "Reservistenkonzeption setzt auf persönliches Engagement," at *www.reserveoffizier-bundeswehr.de/ 01DB040100000001/vwContentByKey/W269GBWU534INFODE*.

112. *Bundeswehr Reservist Concept*, pp. 10, 18.

113. Struck, *Verteidigungspolitische Richtlinien für den Geschäftsbereich des Bundesministers der Verteidigung*, article 80.

114. "Beorderungsunabhängige, freiwillige Reservistenarbeit, ResArb," May 9, 2006, at *reservisten.bundeswehr.de/ 01DB171000000001/Docname/Reservistenarbeit_Home*.

115. *Bundeswehr Reservist Concept*, pp. 12-14.

116. *Ibid.*, p. 12.

117. *Ibid.*, p. 20.

118. de Jong, *NATO's Reserve Forces*, p. 40.

119. *Bundeswehr Reservist Concept*, pp. 21-22.

120. NATO National Reserve Forces Committee "National Reserve Forces Status: Canada," June 23, 2004, pp. 2-3, at *www. nato.int/nrfc/database/canada.pdf*.

121. National Audit Office, *Ministry of Defence Reserve Forces*, London: The Stationary Office, March 28, 2006, p. 52.

122. For details on the size and order of battle for each Service component, see The International Institute for Strategic Studies, *The Military Balance: 2007*, London: Routledge, 2007, p. 26.

123. Bill Graham, *2004-2005 Report on Plans and Priorities*, Department of National Defence, 2005, p. 31.

124. *Ibid.*, p. 32.

125. NATO National Reserve Forces Committee, "National Reserve Forces Status: Canada," p. 1.

126. Air Force Public Affairs. Department of National Defence, "Canadian Forces Reserve Structure," June 16, 2004, at *www.airforce.forces.ca/air_reserve/organization/cf_structure_e.asp.*

127. Department of National Defence, "Canadian Rangers," November 4, 2005, at *www.rangers.dnDCa/pubs/rangers/intro_e.asp.*

128. Assistant Deputy Minister, Public Affairs, Department of National Defence, "Backgrounder: The Reserve Force and Reserve Classes of Service," May 2, 2002, at *www.forces.gc.ca/site/newsroom/view_news_e.asp?id=396.*

129. David Collenette, *Defence White Paper*, Ottawa: Department of National Defence, 1994, at *www.forces.gc.ca/site/Minister/eng/94wpaper/seven_e.html.*

130. Patrick Crofton, Standing Committee on National Defence, "First Report on the White Paper on National Defence," Ottawa: Queen's Printer, 1988, pp. 1-2.

131. Department of National Defence, *Challenge and Commitment: A Defence Policy for Canada*, Ottawa: Canadian Government Publishing Centre, 1987, p. 65.

132. Directorate of Reserves, "Reserve Training Courses," April 20, 2004, at *www.vcds.forces.gc.ca/dres/pubs/training_e.asp.*

133. *Ibid.*

134. Department of National Defence, "Selected Canadian Primary Reservists Entitled to Serve within UK Reserve Units," October 18, 2005, at *www.vcds.forces.gc.ca/dres/pubs/compensation/newMOU_e.asp.*

135. Christopher Lamoureux, "USAWC Strategy Research Project: An Evaluation of the Canadian-US Armies Reserve

Relationship." *Journal of Military and Strategic Studies*, Vol.7, No. 2, Winter 2004, at *www.ciaonet.org/olj/jmss/jmss_2004/v7n2/jmss_v7n2c.pdf*.

136. John A. Fraser, "In Service of The Nation: Canada's Citizen Soldiers for the 21st Century," Ottawa: Department of National Defence, 2000, at *www.forces.gc.ca/site/reports/Fraser/cover_e.asp.*

137. These initiatives are described in more detail in R. R. Henault, *A Time For Transformation: Annual Report of the Chief of the Defence Staff, 2002-2003*, Ottawa: 2003, pp. 61-62.

138. NATO National Reserve Forces Committee "National Reserve Forces Status: Canada," p. 2.

139. Department of National Defence, "LFRR Backgrounder," March 2, 2005, at *www.army.forces.gc.ca/lf/English/9_3_1.asp*.

140. Department of Foreign Affairs and International Trade, *Canada's International Policy Statement: A Role of Pride and Influence in the World* (Ottawa, 2005) *http://geo.international.gc.ca/cip-pic/ips/ips-overview4-en.aspx;* and *http://geo.international.gc.ca/cip-pic/ips/ips-overview5-en.aspx*.

141. John Beaumont, *Australian Defence: Sources and Statistics*, Vol. VI, *The Australian Centenary History of Defence*, South Melbourne, Australia: Oxford University Press, 2001, p. 393.

142 For a survey of Australian involvement in American-led military operations, see Paul Dibb, "U.S.-Australia Alliance Relations: An Australian View," *Strategic Forum*, No. 216, August 2005, at *www.ndu.edu/inss/Strforum/SF216/sf_216_web.pdf#search='U.S.Australia percent20Alliance percent20Relations percent3A percent20An percent20Australian percent20View'*.

143. Department of Defence, "Australian Defence Force Operations," May 10, 2006, at *www.defence.gov.au/globalops.cfm*.

144. Department of Defence, "What the Reserves Do," August 23, 2005, at *www.defence.gov.au/reserves/What_the_Reserves_do.htm*.

145. Chris Tinkler, "Victoria's Elite in the Firing Line: Taking Aim at the Terrorists," *Sunday Herald Sun*, Melbourne, May 2, 2004.

146. Department of Defence, *Australia's National Security: A Defence Update 2005*, at *www.defence.gov.au/update2005/defence_update_2005.pdf*.

147. The International Institute for Strategic Studies, *The Military Balance: 2007*, London: Routledge, 2007, p. 342.

148. A permanent resident's failure to obtain citizenship will result in termination of their reservist contract.

149. "FAQ Categories: Commitment," at *www.defencejobs.gov. au/default.asp?p=33&IntCatID=12.*

150. "FAQ Categories: Gender Restrictions," at *www.defencejobs. gov.au/default.asp?p=33&IntCatID=9.*

151. "Underage Candidates," at *www.defencejobs.gov.au/default. asp?p=160.*

152. Department of Defence, "Categories of Service," August 23, 2005, at *www.defence.gov.au/reserves/Categories_of_Service.htm.*

153. Department of Defence, "Training Requirements," August 23, 2005, at *www.defence.gov.au/reserves/Training_Requirements. htm.*

154. David Horner, *Making the Australian Defence Force*, Vol. IV, *The Australian Centenary History of Defence*, South Melbourne, Australia: Oxford University Press, 2001, p. 84.

155. "Discover Defence: Army Reserves" at *www.defence.gov. au/discover/fs006.cfm.*

156. National Audit Office, *Ministry of Defence Reserve Forces*, London: The Stationary Office, March 28, 2006, p. 52.

157. Daniel Cotterill, "Protected and Plugged-in the Way to Go," *Weekend Australian*, May 27, 2006, extra edition.

158. Steve Lewis and Patrick Walters, "Army to Get Elite Reserves," *The Australian*, March 24, 2006.

159. Army Headquarters, "The Hardened and Networked Army: More Capable Reserve," at *www.defence.gov.au/army/hna/ default2.htm.*

160. Peter Leahy, "The Australian Army Reserve: Relevant and Ready," *Australian Army Reserve*, Vol. 2, No. 1, 2004, p. 12.

161. Beaumont, *Australian Defence: Sources and Statistics*, p. 394.

162. Department of Defence, *Australian Defence Force Reserves*, Commonwealth of Australia, 2004, section 3.4, at *www.anao.gov.au/ WebSite.nsf/Publications/4A256AE90015F69B4A256A450024D2A9.*

163. Information on the NR is available at "Welcome to the Australian Naval Reserve Online," at *www.navy.gov.au/reserves_new/home/Home.cfm.*

164. For additional information, see "Air Force Reserves," at *www.defence.gov.au/raaf/reserves/index.htm.*

165. Department of Defence, "Office of Reserve Service Protection," August 23, 2005, at *www.defence.gov.au/reserves/Reserve_Service_Protection.htm.*

166. Department of Defence, "Modernisation of the Reserves," August 23, 2005, at *www.defence.gov.au/reserves/Modernisation.htm.* See also Department of Defence, "Relationship between Government, Employers and Reservists all Important," June 20, 2006, at *defencereserves.deadline.net.au/cms_resources/documents/News/ORSPJune2006.doc.*

167. See the helpful table on "Protected Service," in Department of Defence, "Categories of Service" August 25, 2006, at *www.defence.gov.au/reserves/Categories_of_Service.htm.*

168. Department of Defence, "Public Sector Leave Policy," August 23, 2005, at *www.defence.gov.au/reserves/Public_Sector_Policy.htm.*

169. Department of Defence, "Employer Support Payments," December 14, 2005, at *www.defence.gov.au/reserves/ESP/*; and the ESP form at *drsc.deadline.net.au/downloads/employer_info/esp_claimform.pdf.*

170. Department of Defence, "Higher Employer Support Payments for Defence Health Professionals," July 3, 2006, at *defencereserves.deadline.net.au/cms_resources/documents/News/MediaReleaseESPHealthProfessionals4Jul06.DOC.*

171. Department of Defence, "What is the DRSC?: Overview," at *drsc.deadline.net.au/asp/what_overview.asp.*

172. "Training Philosophy by Wing Commander Carl Schiller, CSM," at *www.defence.gov.au/raaf/reserves/join/training.htm.*

173. Directorate of Strategic Personnel Planning and Research, *2004 Australian Defence Force Reserves: Attitude Survey Report,* February 2005, p. 14, at *www.defence.gov.au/reserves/docs/2004 percent20Reserve percent20Attitude percent20Survey.pdf.*

174. Department of Defence, *Defence Annual Report 2003-04,* Commonwealth of Australia, 2004, p. 273, at *www.defence.gov.au/budget/03-04/dar/download/full.pdf.*

175. Ian McPhedran, "Army Reserve Facing a Numbers Crisis," *Hobart Mercury*, October 12, 2005.

176. Nick Squires, "Army Fights Losing Battle against Underfunding," *South China Morning Post*, February 2, 2005.

177. Peter Charlton, "Reserve Runs Low," *The Courier Mail*, Queensland, Australia, October 1, 2005; and "Audit Report— Australian Defence Force Reserves" at *www.anao.gov.au/WebSite. nsf/Publications/4A256AE90015F69B4A256A450024D2A9*.

178. For a description, see Ian McPhedran, "Pay Students for Military Service Plan," *Daily Telegraph*, Sydney, October 12, 2005.

179. "Executive Summary," *The Cost of Defence: ASPI Defence Budget Brief 2006-2007*, Barton: Australian Strategic Policy Institute, May 2006, at *www.aspi.org.au/programsBudget.cfm#*.

180. Lewis and Walters.

181. Department of Defense, *Australia's National Security: A Defence Update 2007* (2007), p. 58, *http://www.defence.gov.au/ ans/2007/pdf/Defence_update.pdf*.

182. "Executive Summary," *The Cost of Defence: ASPI Defence Budget Brief 2006-2007*, Barton: Australian Strategic Policy Institute, May 2006, at *http://www.aspi.org.au/programsBudget.cfm#*.

183. Lewis and Walters, "Army to Get Elite Reserves."

184. Office of the U.S. Secretary of Defense, *Annual Report to Congress: Military Power of the People's Republic of China 2006*, Washington, DC: Department of Defense, 2006, p. i, at *www. dod.mil/pubs/pdfs/China percent20Report percent202006.pdf*. For a comprehensive assessment of China's military buildup, see David Shambaugh, "China's Military Modernization: Making Steady and Surprising Progress," in *Strategic Asia 2005-06: Military Modernization in an Era of Uncertainty*, Seattle, WA: National Bureau of Asian Research, 2005, pp. 67-103.

185. "Strengthening building of contingent reserve officers according to law," *Renmin ribao*, May 15, 1995, p. 3, in *Foreign Broadcast Information Service* (FBIS)-CHI, May 23, 1995, pp. 41-42, cited in "Demobilization," *China's Military in Transition*, David Shambaugh and Richard H. Yang, eds., New York: Oxford University Press, 1997, p. 93.

186. Tai Ming Cheung, "The Streamlining of the Chinese Armed Forces: Towards a More High-Tech and Mobile Capability," *Royal*

United Services Institute Chinese Military Update, Vol. 1, No. 4, September 2003, p. 5.

187. U.S. Secretary of Defense, *Military Power of the People's Republic of China 2006*, p. 2.

188. Xinhui, "People's Liberation Army's Reserve Forces, A Preliminary Study: Conclusion," *China Defense.com*, February 2, 2006, at *www.china-defense.com/pla/pla_reserve*.

189. Solomon Karmel, *China and the People's Liberation Army: Great Power or Struggling Developing State*, New York: St. Martin's Press, 2000, p. 59.

190. James C. Mulvenon, "The PLA's Army Struggle for Identity," in Stephen J. Flanagan and Michael E. Marti, eds., *The People's Liberation Army and China in Transition*, Washington, DC: National Defense University Press, 2003, p. 115.

191. For the lower estimate, see Cliff Crane *et al.*, *Modernizing China's Military: Opportunities and Constraints*, Santa Monica, CA: RAND, 2005, p. 38; the higher estimate is from The International Institute for Strategic Studies, *The Military Balance: 2007*, London: Routledge, 2007, pp. 264-265.

192. Dennis J. Blasko, *The Chinese Army Today: Tradition and Transformation for the 21st Century*, New York: Routledge, 2006, pp. 86-87.

193. Blasko, p. 22. The PLA ground forces rely more on unit rather than individual replacement.

194. Catherine Armitage, "Workforce to Be Reckoned With," *The Australian*, August 19, 2002.

195. Nan Li, "PLA Conservative Nationalism," in Stephen J. Flanagan and Michael E. Marti, eds., *The People's Liberation Army and China in Transition*, Washington, DC: National Defense University Press, 2003, p. 79.

196. Information Office of the State Council of the People's Republic of China, *China's National Defense in 2004*, Beijing: December 2004, chapter 5, at *www.china.org.cn/e-white/20041227/V.htm#1*; and Xinhui, "People's Liberation Army's Reserve Forces."

197. Ka Po Ng, *Interpreting China's Military Power*, London: Frank Cass: 2005, p. 144.

198. Dennis J. Blasko, "Chinese Army Modernization: An Overview," *Military Review*, September-October 2005, p. 71.

199. People's Republic of China, *China's National Defense in 2004*, chapter 6, at *www.china.org.cn/e-white/20041227/VI.htm#1*.

200. *Ibid.*

201. Timothy L. Thomas, "China's Electronic Strategies," *Military Review*, May-June 2001, at *fmso.leavenworth.army.mil/documents/china_electric/china_electric.htm*.

202. U.S. Secretary of Defense, *Military Power of the People's Republic of China 2006*, p. 35.

203. People's Republic of China, *China's National Defense in 2004*, chapter 8, at *www.china.org.cn/e-white/20041227/VIII.htm*.

204. Dennis Blasko, "People's Liberation Army Ground Forces: Moving into the 21st Century," *Royal United Services Institute Chinese Military Update*, Vol. 1, No. 2, July 2003, p. 7.

205. People's Republic of China, *China's National Defense in 2000*, chapter 3, at *www.china.org.cn/e-white/2000/20-4.htm*.

206. Harvey W. Nelsen, *The Chinese Military System: An Organizational Study of the Chinese People's Liberation Army*, second edition, Boulder, CO: Westview Press, 1981, pp. 177-183; and William R. Heaton, Jr., "The People's Republic of China," in *The Defense Policies of Nations: A Comparative Study*, third edition, Douglas J. Murray and Paul R. Viotti, eds., Baltimore: Johns Hopkins University Press, 1994, p. 395.

207. Nicolas Becquelin, "Xinjiang in the Nineties," *The China Journal*, No. 44, July 2000, pp. 65-90.

208. "Militia and Reserve Forces," January 22, 2005, at *www.sinodefense.com/army/orbat/reserve.asp*.

209. "PLA Reserve Forces," January 28, 2006, at *www.globalsecurity.org/military/world/china/pla-reserve.htm*.

210. Blasko, *Chinese Army Today*, p. 18; and David Shambaugh, "The People's Liberation Army and the People's Republic at 50: Reform at Last," *The China Quarterly*, No. 59, 1999, pp. 663-664.

211. For a detailed PAP order of battle, see "People's Armed Police," January 22, 2005, at *www.sinodefence.com/army/orbat/pap.asp*.

212. Blasko, *Chinese Army Today*, p. 87.

213. Crane *et al.*, *Modernizing China's Military*, pp. 129-131.

214. Blasko, *Chinese Army Today*, pp. 23, 87.

215. Other possible roles of the militia in wartime are discussed in "PLA Reserve Forces," April 27, 2005, at *www.globalsecurity.org/ military/world/china/pla-reserve.htm*.

216. Yamaguchi Noboru, "Japanese Adjustments to the Security Alliance with the United States: Evolution of Policy on the Roles of the Self-Defense Force," in Michael H. Armacost and Daniel I. Okimoto, eds., *The Future of America's Alliances in Northeast Asia*, Washington, DC: Brookings Institution, 2004, p. 88.

217. Thomas Wilborn, *Japan's Self-Defense Forces: What Dangers to Northeast Asia?* Carlisle, PA: *Strategic Studies Institute*, 1994, p. 21.

218. For an analysis of the restrictions, see Christopher Hughes, *Japan's Security Agenda: Military, Economic & Environmental Dimensions*, Boulder, CO: Lynne Rienner, 2004, pp. 161-162.

219. For a comprehensive list of Japan's participation in U.N. peacekeeping operations during the 1990s, see Akiko Fukushima, "UN Peacekeeping Operations and Japan's Role in Retrospect and Prospect: A Possible U.S.-Japan Cooperation," in *Reinventing the Alliance: U.S.-Japan Security Partnership in an Era of Change*, G. John Ikenberry and Takashi Inoguchi, eds., New York: Palgrave MacMillan, 2003, pp. 239-242.

220. Office of Assistant Secretary of Defense, Public Affairs, "Completion of the Review of the Guidelines for U.S.-Japan Defense Cooperation," September 23, 1997, at *www.defenselink. mil/news/Sep1997/b09231997_bt50797b.html*.

221. The details of the legislation are described in The International Institute for Strategic Studies, *Strategic Survey 2002/3*, London: Oxford University Press, 2003, p. 255. Japan's resulting military deployments in Afghanistan and Iraq are discussed in Steven R. Saunders, *Asian Security Handbook: Terrorism and the New Security Environment*, third edition, William M. Carpenter and David G. Wiencek, eds., Armonk, NY: M. E. Sharp, 2005, pp. 151-152.

222. U.S. Department of State, "Joint Statement of the U.S.-Japan Security Consultative Committee," February 19, 2005, at *www.state.gov/r/pa/prs/ps/2005/42490.htm*.

223. Asia-Pacific Area Network, "Exercise Cobra Gold 06 History," May 15, 2006, at *www.apan-info.net/cobragold/fullstory. asp?id=117*.

224. Nicholas Szechenyi, "A Turning Point for Japan's Self-Defense Forces," *The Washington Quarterly*, Vol. 29, No. 4, Autumn 2006, pp. 139-150. For details on the SDF order of battle, see The International Institute for Strategic Studies, *The Military Balance, 2005/6*, London: Routledge, 2005, pp. 279-282. Japan's robust air and naval power projection capacity is highlighted in Jennifer M. Lind, "Pacifism or Passing the Buck?: Testing Theories of Japanese Security Policy," *International Security*, Vol. 29, No. 1, Summer 2004, pp. 94-101.

225. For a discussion of the move to revise the constitution, see Haruko Satoh, "Japan Seeks Its Constitutional Soul," *Far Eastern Economic Review*, Vol. 168, No. 7, July/August 2005, pp. 30-34.

226. Tony Perry and Bruce Wallace, "Japanese Troops Shore Up Skills," *Los Angeles Times*, January 13, 2006.

227. "December 2005 Nikkei Regular Telephone Opinion Poll," December 23-25, 2005, question 10, at *www.mansfieldfdn.org/polls/poll-05-13.htm*.

228. Morton I. Abramowitz, Funabashi Yoichi, and Wang Jisi, *China-Japan-U.S. Relations: Meeting New Challenges*, Tokyo: Japan Center for International Exchange, 2002, p. 50.

229. Japan Defense Agency, *Defense of Japan 2005*, "Summary/Tentative Translation," p. 13, at *www.jda.go.jp/e/index_.htm*.

230. "National Defense Program Guideline FY 2005," "Provisional Translation," December 10, 2004, at *www.kantei.go.jp/foreign/policy/2004/1210taikou_e.html*.

231. The International Institute for Strategic Studies, *The Military Balance: 2007*, London: Routledge, 2007, pp. 273-275. See also *www.jda.go.jp/j/defense/yobiji/yobiji.htm*.

232. For more information on the differences between the three reserve components see Japan Defense Agency, *Defense of Japan 2001*, Tokyo, 2001, pp. 147-149; Japan Defense Agency, *Defense of Japan 2005*, Tokyo, 2005, pp. 73-74; Japan Defense Agency, *Defense of Japan 2006*, Tokyo, 2006, chapter 6, pp. 10-11; and *www.jda.go.jp/j/defense/yobiji/hikaku.htm*.

233. Japan Ministry of Defense, *Defense of Japan 2007* (Tokyo, 2007), part 3, chapter 1, p. 39, note 56, at *http://www.mod.go.jp/e/publ/w_paper/index.html*.

234. Japan Ministry of Defense, *Defense of Japan 2007* (Tokyo, 2007), part 3, chapter 4, p. 3, at *http://www.mod.go.jp/e/publ/w_paper/index.html*.

235. "Protecting Japan: Are Reserves Really Ready to Go?" *The Daily Yomiuri*, Tokyo, January 10, 2004; and Japan Defense Agency, *Defense of Japan 2001*, Tokyo, 2001, p. 147.

236. *Ibid.*

237. See, for example, Japan Defense Agency, "Results of Opinion Poll on SDF and Defense Issues," *Japan Defense Focus*, No. 2, July 2006, p. 3.

238. In October 2005, the U.S.-Japan Security Consultative Committee issued a report that identified the following possible areas for improved bilateral defense cooperation:

> air defense; ballistic missile defense; counterproliferation operations; counter-terrorism; minesweeping, maritime interdiction, and other operations to maintain the security of maritime traffic; search and rescue operations; intelligence, surveillance and reconnaissance operations, including increasing capabilities and effectiveness of operations by unmanned aerial vehicles and maritime patrol aircraft; humanitarian relief operations; reconstruction assistance operations; peacekeeping operations and capacity building for other nations' peacekeeping efforts; protection of critical infrastructure, including U.S. facilities and areas in Japan; response to attacks by weapons of mass destruction, including disposal and decontamination of WMD; mutual logistics support activities such as supply, maintenance, and transportation; supply cooperation including mutual provision of aerial and maritime refueling; transportation cooperation including expanding and sharing airlift and sealift, including the capability provided by high speed vessels, HSV; transportation, use of facilities, medical support, and other related activities for non-combatant evacuation operations, NEO; and use of seaport and airport facilities, road, water space and airspace, and frequency bands.

"U.S.-Japan Alliance: Transformation and Realignment for the Future," October 29, 2005, at *www.mofa.go.jp/region/n-america/us/security/scc/doc0510.html*.

239. Stuart A. Cohen, "Operational Limitations of Reserve Forces: Lessons of the 1973 War," *Israel Affairs*, Vol. 6, No. 1, Autumn 1999, p. 73.

240. Anthony H. Cordesman, *The Arab-Israeli Military Balance in 2002: Part 3: Trends in National Forces*, Washington, DC: Center for Strategic and International Studies, February 2002, at *www.csis.org/media/csis/pubs/ai_mb_natl_forces[1].pdf*.

241. Gabriel Ben-Dor, Ami Pedahzur, and Badi Hasisi, "Israel's National Security Doctrine under Strain: The Crisis of the Reserve Army," *Armed Forces and Society*, Vol. 28, No. 2, Winter 2002, p. 234.

242. Dafna N. Izraeli, "Paradoxes of Women's Service in the Israel Defense Forces," in Daniel Maman, Eyal Ben-Ari, and Zeev Rosenhek, eds., *Military, State, and Society in Israel: Theoretical and Comparative Perspectives*, New Brunswick, NJ: Transaction Publishers, 2001, p. 211.

243. The International Institute for Strategic Studies, *The Military Balance: 2007*, London: Routledge, 2007, p. 228.

244. Bar Dadon, "The Need for an Economic Model for the IDF Reserves," Institute for Advanced Strategic and Political Studies, May 1999, pp. 5, 9, at *www.iasps.org/policystudies/ps40.pdf*.

245. Gunther E. Rothenberg, *The Anatomy of the Israeli Army*, New York: Hippocrene, 1979, p. 82.

246. Martin Van Creveld, *The Sword and the Olive: A Critical History of the Israeli Defense Force*, New York: Public Affairs, 1998, pp. 114-115.

247. Dadon, p. 7.

248. Dan Horowitz and Edward Luttwak, *The Israeli Army*, London: A. Lane, 1975, p. 203.

249. Efraim Inbar, *Rabin and Israel's National Security*, Washington DC: Woodrow Wilson Center, 1999. p. 66; and Avner Yaniv, *Deterrence Without the Bomb: The Politics of Israeli Strategy*, Lexington, MA: Lexington Books, 1987, p. 76.

250. Emanuel Wald, "*The Wald Report: The Decline of Israeli National Security since 1967*, Tel Aviv: Schoken, 1992, pp. 95-97.

251. Cohen, p. 71.

252. He also compared the IDF to an iceberg, with nine-tenths of the force (the reserves) hidden from view.

253. Dadon, pp. 12-13.

254. Mary Curtius, "Israeli Reservists Protest the Lot of Those Bound by a Sense of Duty," *Los Angeles Times*, April 21, 2001.

255. Haim Watzman, "Reserve Duty in Israel Puts Studying on Hold," *Chronicle of Higher Education*, Vol. 47, No. 15, June 2001, p. 39.

256. Dan Horowitz, "Strategic Limitations of a 'Nation in Arms'," *Armed Forces and Society*, Vol. 13, No. 2, 1987, pp. 282-286.

257. *Ibid.*, p. 287.

258. Dadon, p. 9.

259. Stuart A. Cohen "Portrait of the New Israeli Soldier," *Middle East Review of International Affairs, Vol.*1, No. 4, December 1997, at *meria.idc.ac.il/journal/1997/issue4/jv1n4a3.html*.

260. Chris Demchak, "Numbers or Networks: Social Constructions of Technology and Organization Dilemmas in IDF Modernization," *Armed Forces and Society*, Vol. 23, No. 2, Winter 1996, p. 180.

261. Anthony Cordesman, *Peace and War: The Arab-Israeli Military Balance Enters the 21st Century*, London: Praeger, 2001, p. 187; and "Giving Reservists Their Due," *Jerusalem Post*, July 17, 1997.

262. "Number of Reservists Evading Duty in Territories Up Sharply," *Haaretz*, March 7, 2001.

263. "Israeli Military Chiefs Demand Call Up of Reserves," January 17, 2001, at *www.survivreausida.net/a4636*.

264. Joel Greenberg, "Split Widens Over Israeli Reservists," *New York Times*, February 2, 2002.

265. Yossi Yehoshua, "IDF Reforms Reserve Scheme," October 17, 2005, at *www.ynetnews.com/articles/0,7340,L-3155987,00.html*.

266. Matthew Gutman, "Israel Shrinking its Citizens' Army," *USA Today*, June 5, 2006.

267. Laura King and J. Michael Kennedy, "Israel Begins to Mobilize Reservists," *Los Angeles Times*, July 28, 2006; and Matthew Kalman, "Israeli Army Officer Mourns Death of Fellow Reservists," *Boston Globe*, August 11, 2006.

268. Peter Waldman, "View on the Ground: Israeli Reservists See Disarray in Lebanon," *The Wall Street Journal*, September 1, 2006.

269. See, for example, Rory McCarthy, "Israeli Reserve Soldiers Accuse Government of 'Cold Feet' Over Conflict," *The Guardian*,

August 22, 2006; Rebecca Anna Stoil, "We Were Eager to Serve But the Army Was Not Ready for Us," *Jerusalem Post*, August 23, 2006; and Doug Struck and Tal Zipper, "War Stirs Worry in Israel over State of Military," *Washington Post*, August 19, 2006.

270. Ze'ev Schiff, "Policing in Gaza Has Blunted IDF Fighting Abilities," *Haaretz*, August 22, 2006.

271. Anshel Pfeffer, "Behind the Lines: Thanks to the Reserves," August 11, 2006, at *www.jpost.com/servlet/Satellite?pagename=JPost %2FJPArticle%2FShowFull&cid=1154525851140*.

272. See, for example, Efraim Karsh, "Preoccupied: Has Occupation Hurt the Israeli Army?," *New Republic Online*, September 9, 2006, at *www.tnr.com/doc.mhtml?i=w060904&s=ka rsh090906*; and David Makovsky and Jeffrey White, *Lessons and Implications of the Israel-Hizballah War: A Preliminary Assessment*, Washington, DC: Washington Institute for Near East Policy, October 2006.

273. Amos Harel, "IDF Chief Halutz: I Never Made Use of Soldiers' Blood," *Haaretz*, September 21, 2006.

274. Yaakov Katz, "IDF Report Card," *Jerusalem Post*, August 24, 2006.

275. Dmitri V. Trenin, "Gold Eagle, Red Star," in *The Russian Military: Power and Policy*, Steven E. Miller and Dmitri V. Trenin, eds., Cambridge, MA: MIT Press, 2004, p. 221.

276. Article 63, which enshrined the principles underpinning the 1967 Law on Universal Military Service, as amended. The tsarist heritage is discussed in Ellen Jones, *Red Army and Society: A Sociology of the Soviet Military*, Boston: Allen & Unwin, 1985, pp. 33-35.

277. For details of the various reduced readiness states of most Soviet units, see Christopher Donnelly, *Red Banner: The Soviet Military System in Peace and War*, Coulsdon, Surrey, UK: Jane's Information Group, 1988, pp. 153, 155-157.

278. See the table relating reservists' age category to their service requirement in Harriet Fast Scott and William F. Scott, *The Armed Forces of the USSR*, third edition, Boulder, CO: Westview, 1984, p. 340.

279. Alexandr Golts, "The Russian Volunteer Military — A New Attempt?" *European Security*, Vol. 12, Nos. 3-4, Autumn-Winter 2003, p. 57.

280. Michael Orr, "Reform and the Russian Ground Forces, 1992-2002," in *Russian Military Reform: 1992-2002,* Anne C. Aldis and Roger N. McDermott, eds., London: Frank Cass, 2003, p. 130. See also Pavel K. Baev, "The Russian Army and Chechnya: Victory Instead of Reform," in *The Russian Military into the Twenty-First Century,* Stephen J. Cimbala, ed., London: Frank Cass, 2001, pp. 75-93.

281. For a review of these failed reform efforts, see Peter Baker and Susan Glasser, *Kremlin Rising: Vladimir Putin's Russia and the End of Revolution,* New York: Scribner, 2005, pp. 200-204, 208-213; David J. Betz and Valeriy G. Volkov, "A New Day for the Russian Army?: Reforming the Armed Forces under Yeltsin and Putin," in Aldis and McDermott, pp. 41-59; and Dale R. Herspring, *Russian Civil-Military Relations,* Bloomington: Indiana University Press, 1996, 93-111. When running for reelection as president in 1996, Yeltsin actually signed a decree eliminating the draft by 2000, a measure that the government quickly ignored after the ballot; see Brian D. Taylor, *Politics and the Russian Army Civil-Military Relations, 1689-2000,* New York: Cambridge University Press, 2003, p. 267.

282. An indeterminate number of the employees of the Russian government's other "power agencies" (e.g., the Ministries of Interior, Justice, Emergency Situations, or the Federal Security Service) also could assist with low-intensity operations such as managing domestic emergencies. For more on these complements, see Alexei G. Arbatov, "Military Reform: From Crisis to Stagnation," in *The Russian Military: Power and Policy,* Steven E. Miller and Dmitri V. Trenin, eds., Cambridge, MA: MIT Press, 2004, pp. 102-103; and Viktor Litovkin, "Are Russia's Armed Forces Ready to Cope with New Challenges," *Vremya MN,* No. 78, June 2003, reprinted in *CDI Russia Weekly,* No. 262, at *www.cdi. org/russia/262-14.cfm.*

283. Nikolay Poroskov, "Prizyv uslyshan," *Vremya Novostey,* July 11, 2006.

284. See, for example, his interview with Dmitri Litovkin in *Izvestia,* March 28, 2006.

285. The gruesome figures are reviewed in Nicholas Eberstadt, "Russia's Demographic Straightjacket," *SAIS Review,* Vol. 24, No. 2, Summer-Fall 2004, pp. 9-25. Patricio V. Marquez, *Dying Too Young — Addressing Premature Mortality and Ill Health Due To Non-Communicable Diseases and Injuries in the Russian Federation:*

Summary, Washington, DC: World Bank, 2005, at *siteresources. worldbank.org/INTECA/Resources/Dying_too_Young_Summary_ UPDATED_Oct_19.pdf*. The consequences for Russia's defense manning policies of these problems is discussed in Judyth Twigg, "National Security Implications of Russia's Health and Demographic Crisis," *PONARS Policy Memo* No. 360, November 2004, at *www.csis.org/media/csis/pubs/pm_0360.pdf/*.

286. Mark Galeotti, "Brutality Threatens Russia's Military Effectiveness," *Jane's Intelligence Review*, Vol. 16, No. 12, December 2004, pp. 46-47.

287. Roger McDermott, "Russian Military Plagued by Falling Conscript Standards," *Eurasia Daily Monitor*, Vol. 1, No. 65, August 3, 2004, at *www.jamestown.org/publications_details.php?volume_ id=401&issue_id=3035&article_id=2368343*.

288. Mark McDonald, "Russian Draft Collects `Bums, Real Scum' as Most Defer Dangerous Military Posts," Knight Ridder Newspapers, March 30, 2005, at *www.ransac.org/Projects percent20andpercent20Publications/News/Nuclearpercent20News/ 2005/331200514111PM.html*.

289. See, for example, his interview with Nikolay Zyatkov in "Defence Minister Sergey Ivanov: We Have an Army of Workers and Peasants," *Argumenti i Fakti*, March 30, 2005.

290. For a poignant example, see Gregory Katz, "A Russian Soldier's Story," *Atlantic Monthly*, June 2006, at *www.theatlantic. com/doc/prem/200606/russian-soldier*; reproduced at *www. strategypage.com/messageboards/messages/47-2094.asp*.

291. Theodore P. Gerber and Sarah E. Mendelson, "Strong Public Support for Military Reform in Russia," *PONARS Policy Memo*, No. 288, May 2003, at *www.csis.org/media/csis/pubs/pm_0288. pdf*.

292. Fred Weir, "In Russia, An Army of Deserters," *Christian Science Monitor*, September 30, 2002.

293. Leonid Polyakov, "Military Reforms in Russia," in *Toward an Understanding of Russia: New European Perspectives*, Janusz Bugajski, ed., New York: Council on Foreign Relations, 2002, p. 81.

294. See, for example, Ivanov's comments in Nalatia Kalashnikova, "The Peace-Time Burden," *Itogi*, No. 15, April 12, 2005, pp. 30-34; and Eugene B. Rumer and Celeste A. Wallander,

"Russia: Power in Weakness?" *The Washington Quarterly*, Vol. 27, No. 1, Winter 2003-04, pp. 62-63.

295. Leon Aron, "The Battle over the Draft," *AEI Russian Outlook*, Summer 2005, at *www.aei.org/publications/pubID.22914/ pub_detail.asp*; and Andrew L. Spirak and William Alex Pridemore, "Corruption and Reforms in the Russian Army," *Problems of Post Communism*, November/December 2004, pp. 33-43.

296. Richard Sakwa, *Russian Politics and Society*, third edition, London: Routledge, 2002, p. 307.

297. Mark Galeotti, "Putin's Russian Legacy," *Jane's Intelligence Review*, Vol. 16, No. 3, March 2004, p. 55. Ivanov continues to reaffirm these force goals; see RIA Novosti, "Defense Minister Outlines Future of Russian Military," March 28, 2006, at *en.rian. ru/russia/20060328/44900218.html*.

298. RIA Novosti, "Russia's Army Will Be Reduced to 1 Mln By 2016—Army Chief," May 10, 2006, at *www.rusnet.nl/ news/2006/05/11/currentaffairs01.shtml*.

299. Ivan Safronov, "Moskva formiruet brigadu dlya sovmestnix deystviy s NATO," *Kommersant*, April 14, 2004; and "Meeting of NATO-Russia Council with Military Representatives," March 15, 2005, IMS Press Advisory, March 18, 2005, available at *www.nato. int/ims/news/2005/n050318e.htm*.

300. Lyubov Pronina, "Russian Military's Combat Potential Unrealized," *Defense News*, December 13, 2004, p. 14.

301. Nikolay Poroskov, "Prizyv uslyshan," *Vremya Novostey*, July 11, 2006.

302. See, for example, Alexei Arbatov, "What Kind of Army Does Russia Need?: The Contours of the Russian Military Reform," *Russia in Global Affairs*, No. 1, January-March 2003, at *eng.globalaffairs.ru/numbers/2/457.html*.

303. Alexander Golts, "Military Reform in Russia and the Global War Against Terrorism," *Journal of Slavic Military Studies*, Vol. 17, No. 1, March 2004, p. 40.

304. Nikolai Poroskov, "Partisani Vozbrashchayutsya," *Vremya Novostei*, February 16, 2005.

305. Viktor Litovkin, "Army Reserve: Not yet 'Individual' or 'Ready'," September 15, 2006, at *en.rian.ru/ analysis/20060915/53934431.html*.

306. "Russia," *Defense & Foreign Affairs Handbook*, fifteenth edition, Washington, DC: International Strategic Studies Association, 2004, p. 1452.

307. Zyatkov.

308. Viktor Litovkin, "An Army Without Patriots: Why the Young Don't Want To Serve in Russia's Armed Forces," *Russia Profile*, Vol. 2, No. 8, October 2005, p. 1.

309. The International Institute for Strategic Studies, *The Military Balance: 2006*, London: Routledge, 2006, p. 154.

310. For more on this concept, see Charles C. Moskos, John Allen Williams, and David R. Segal, eds., *The Postmodern Military: Armed Forces after the Cold War*, New York: Oxford University Press, 2000.

311. George W. Bush, *The National Security Strategy of the United States of America*, Washington, DC: March 2006, pp. 35-42.

312. Chairman of the Joint Chiefs of Staff, *The National Military Strategy of the United States of America*, Washington, DC: 2004, p. 2.

313. U.S. Department of Defense, *The National Defense Strategy of the United States of America*, Washington, DC: March 2005, pp. 10, 15.

314. *Quadrennial Defense Review Report*, pp. 14-15.

315. Other U.S. government agencies have adopted similar measures; see Bradley Graham, "Foreign-Language Learning Promoted," *Washington Post*, January 6, 2006.

316. Donald C. Winter, "SECNAV Posture Statement: Providing the Right Force for the Nation Today . . . While Preparing for the Uncertainties of Tomorrow," March 2006, p. 11, at *www.navy.mil/ navydata/people/secnav/winter/secnav_posture_statement.pdf#search= %22SECNAV%20Posture%20Statement%22*.

317. Cited in Stephen Trimble, "USN Seeks to Widen its Concept of 'Seapower'," *Jane's Defence Weekly*, June 21, 2006, p. 4.

318. Kurt Campbell and Richard Weitz, "The Limits of U.S.-China Military Cooperation: Lessons from 1995-1999," *The Washington* Quarterly, Vol. 29, No. 1, Winter 2005, pp. 169-186.

319. *Quadrennial Defense Review Report*, pp. 27-35.

320. Andrew Cottey and Anthony Forster, *Reshaping Defence Diplomacy: New Roles for Military Cooperation and Assistance*,

Adelphi Paper no. 365, New York: Oxford University Press, 2004, p. 28.

321. Additional information on the NGB SPPs, as well as recommendations on how to improve them, can be found in Jefferson P. Marquis *et al.*, *Assessing the Value of U.S. Army International Activities*, Santa Monica, CA: RAND, 2006, pp. 84-90.

322. Neil King, Jr., and Greg Jaffe, "U.S. Sets New Mission for Keeping the Peace," *Wall Street Journal*, January 3, 2006.

323. Department of Defense Directive 3000.05, "SUBJECT: Military Support for Stability, Security, Transition, and Reconstruction (SSTR) Operations," November 28, 2005, signed by Acting Under Secretary of Defense Gordon England, at *www.dtic.mil/whs/directives/corres/pdf/d300005_112805/d300005p.pdf*.

324. *Quadrennial Defense Review Report*, p. 88. See also Tom Bowman, "Military Aims To Bolster Language Skills," *Baltimore Sun*, January 2, 2006.

325. A range of possible initiatives are offered in Clark A. Murdock *et al.*, *U.S. Government and Defense Reform for a New Strategic Era*, Washington, DC: Center for Strategic and International Studies, July 2005, especially chapter 3.

326. *Quadrennial Defense Review Report*, p. 77.

327. For a description of the ESGR's history and objectives see Bob Hollingsworth, "The National Committee for Employer Support of the Guard and Reserve," *Military Review*, May-June 2004, pp. 49-52; and the organization's website at *www.esgr.org/*.

328. Some recent U.S. reserve component recruitment initiatives are discussed in Ann Scott Tyson, "Army Guard Refilling Its Ranks," *Washington Post*, March 12, 2006.

329. For a discussion of this concept, see Dennis M. McCarthy, "The Continuum of Reserve Service," *Joint Forces Quarterly*, No. 36, December 2004, pp. 30-35.

330. Data on the civilian-military salary differentials and related issues can be found in Matt Kelley, "Contractors, Military in 'Bidding War'," *USA Today*, July 31, 2005; and Peter W. Singer, *Corporate Warriors: The Rise of the Privatized Military Industry*, Ithaca, NY: Cornell University Press, 2004. GAO investigators found they could not conclusively determine whether or not the expanded use of private security providers appears to be increasing attrition

among military personnel. See U.S. Government Accountability Office, *Rebuilding Iraq: Actions Needed to Improve Use of Private Security Providers*, Washington, DC: July 2005, pp. 35-38.

331. Peter Singer, "Outsourcing War," *Foreign Affairs*, Vol. 119, No. 84, March/April 2005, p. 123.

332. According to the Albert C. Zapanta, Chairman of the Reserve Forces Policy Board: "Today, the Total Force is comprised of the Active and Reserve components, Department of Defense civilians, and the civilian contractor workforce." "Transforming Reserve Forces," *Joint Forces Quarterly*, No. 36, December 2004, p. 64.

333. U.S. Department of Defense, "Contractor Personnel Authorized to Accompany the U.S. Armed Forces," Instruction No. 3020.41, October 3, 2005, at *www.fas.org/irp/doddir/dod/i3020_4 1.pdf#search=%22Contractor%20Personnel%20Authorized%20to%2 0Accompany%20the%20U.S.%20Armed%20Forces%22*.

334. Wormuth *et al.*, *The Future of the National Guard and Reserves*, p. 60.

ABOUT THE AUTHOR

RICHARD WEITZ is a Senior Fellow and Director of Program Management at the Hudson Institute, where he analyzes diverse national and international security issues. His current areas of research include defense reform, counterterrorism, homeland security, and U.S. policies towards Europe, the former Soviet Union, Asia, and the Middle East. Dr. Weitz has written extensively in such journals as *The National Interest, The Washington Quarterly, NATO Review, Studies in Conflict and Terrorism, Defense Concepts,* and *The Journal of Strategic Studies.* His commentaries have appeared in the *International Herald Tribune, Baltimore Sun, The Washington Times,* the *Wall Street Journal* (Europe), and many Internet-based publications. Dr. Weitz is a graduate of Harvard College (B.A. with Highest Honors in Government), the London School of Economics (M.Sc. in International Relations), Oxford University (M.Phil. in Politics), and Harvard University (Ph.D. in Political Science).